Rest
The Unforced Rhythm
of
Grace

SIBANGILIZWE NDLOVU

---

7 The ***old way***, with laws etched in stone, ***led to death***, though it began with such glory that the people of Israel could not bear to look at Moses' face. For his face shone with the glory of God, even though the brightness was ***already fading away.***

8 Shouldn't we expect far greater glory under the new way, now that the Holy Spirit is giving life? 9 If the old way, which brings condemnation, was glorious, ***how much more glorious is the new way, which makes us right with God!***

2 Corinthians 3:7-9 New Living translation

Copyright © 2021 PastorSbanga.Com

Published by PastorSbanga.Com

ISBN: 978-0-6451486-0-2

All rights reserved

This book or parts thereof may not be reproduced in any form, stored in any retrieval system, or transmitted in any form by any means—electronic, mechanical, photocopy, recording, or otherwise—without prior written permission of the publisher, except for brief quotations for use in public ministry.

All Scripture Quotations have been highlighted with the version of the Bible used, abbreviated as shown below. Used by permission.

NIV – New International Version Copyright Holy Bible, New International Version®, NIV® Copyright © 1973, 1978, 1984, 2011 by Biblica, Inc.® Used by permission. All rights reserved worldwide.

KJV – King James Version

NLT –Scripture quotations are taken from the Holy Bible, New Living Translation, copyright ©1996, 2004, 2007

BSB – Berean Study Bible (BSB) © 2016 by Bible Hub and Berean Bible

ASV – American Standard Version

DEDICATION

This book is dedicated to my daddy God, whose kindness leads us to repentance, my Saviour Jesus Christ, my comforter the Great Holy Spirit and to everyone who is tired of religion, has a hunger, thirst and desire to live a liberated and fulfilling life in Christ.

Table of Contents

1 | Lenses of Grace 1
2 | Old and New Covenant 11
3 | Understanding the New Covenant 23
4 | Jesus Our Rest 32
5 | Unrest and Unbelief 44
6 | Two Dimensions of Rest 53
7 | Finding Rest for your soul 66
8 | A Psalm of Rest 74
9 | The Sabbath Rest 83
10| Restful Prayer 92
11 | Effortless Testimonies 104
12 | Restful Warfare 119
13 | Eternally Secure in Christ 129
14 | Grace, Rest and Holiness 136
15 | Rest in God's love 144
16 | Stop Trying, Rest 158

ACKNOWLEDGEMENT

I would like to acknowledge the following people who have cheered me on to finally publish this book.

My wife Thembi and my 3 children Zee, Lerato and Lomusa for your affectionate love for the Lord in your individual capacities and serving in our local church.

Crispen Chamunyonga, QUT Lecturer and former congregant of the late Dr. Myles Munroe. You motivated me the last five years to write this book and also went on to review it in greater detail. You are a true brother in Christ.

Pastor Stan Makumbe, Rev. N Mhlanga of Glory Temple Ministries and several pastors and leaders who took their time to read my script and return constructive doctrinal insight. Thank you very much.

Dr. Creflo & Pastor Taffi Dollar from Creflo Dollar Ministries. When you visited the Gold Coast, QLD in Australia in October 2017, you took time to prophesy, minister and encourage me to keep teaching this Grace message regardless of the challenges I faced. Thank you.

Lastly, my local church community, The Charis Church in Wynnum, QLD Australia. You are a living testimony of what this book is all about.

1 | LENSES OF GRACE

The Message Bible portrays what Jesus says in Matthew 11:28-30 in extra-ordinary fashion, in a way that anyone can understand. If this describes you, then this is your book. Jesus says:

"Are you tired? Worn out? Burned out on religion? Come to me. Get away with me and you'll recover your life. I'll show you how to take a real rest. Walk with me and work with me—watch how I do it. Learn the unforced rhythms of grace. I won't lay anything heavy or ill-fitting on you. Keep company with me and you'll learn to live freely and lightly."

This is what this book is about – recovering your life, to live freely and lightly, by learning the unforced rhythms of grace. A rhythm of grace refers to a regular, free and repeated pattern of a life of favor upon favor! This kind of life gives you rest because of what Jesus did on the cross. 1 Corinthians 7:23NLT says, 'God **paid** a high price for you, so don't be enslaved by the world.' Galatians 5:1NLT also affirms this saying 'So Christ **has** truly set us free. Now make sure that you **stay free**, and don't get tied up again in slavery **to the law**.' You notice these two verses give us past tense of what has already been done. Your purchase price has been paid – done! Being set free has been done too – past tense. As for you just 'stay free' and don't be enslaved 'to the law' again. This is the life of rest God wants for you – free, light, unforced. How is this done, how do you stay free? This is the reason this book has been written; it will transform your life.

When I first taught on rest as an unforced rhythm of grace at a church I once pastored, there was an uproar of disapproval. That took me by surprise because rest was really the Good News that our Lord Jesus came to give a restless, lost world. He came to help the weary and heavy laden, so that He may give them rest. Rest is truly the answer the world, burdened with sin and failing human effort, needed so badly.

Questions flooded after that service as well-meaning believers started asking questions like "so we don't have to go to work? We just have to sit down…no ways" they argued. It did make heaps of sense, but what it meant for me was there was a lot of more depth into the subject of rest than what I had presented in my sermon. Also, that rest was being confused with inactivity, laziness or relaxation. Teaching any of those would be criminal in that it conflicts with scriptures such as "The one who is unwilling to work shall not eat" (2 Thessalonians 3:10).

Secondly, I noted that it was beyond just understanding the teaching of rest that day, it was a belief system that had been entrenched in their souls which made it hard to accept certain liberating teachings of the true nature of God's love. A child born and raised under unloving parents will always be sceptical when true love shows up. This was my situation when I presented this life-changing message. Wrong beliefs result in wrong actions that produce wrong outcomes in life.

I had pastored this church for eight years, a church I had planted. The Lord had brought me to this glorious understanding of His person as a Father overflowing with love and mercy. He uniquely instructed me to minister the gospel message of His Grace, His Love and His Glory into great depths as He initially intended. This was a total difference to what I had understood for many years. I had known God as a God who wants to punish unbelievers and send them to hell, yet God is looking out for sinners to save them from hell. I had understood Him as a God who was quick to curse if you don't align with his strict rules of holiness. I defended that thought about God with a passion until He appeared to me and flooded my soul with His immeasurable love and revelation of the fulness of His person. For the first time, I was introduced to His unmerited, unearned and undeserved favour - His grace, and my life has never been the same since.

Unfortunately for my case, I lost the church I had planted and pastored. I lost friends. I lost income. I lost my reputation. Fellow pastors and ministers turned their backs on me. I became a laughing stock and examples of me were used everywhere, because of this message of God's love. I don't regret all this loss. The apostle Paul considered all things as dung that he could know Christ. In me was this valuable life I couldn't trade for anything. This book is the first of many resources where I explain the deep liberating truths of God's Word in the life of a new creation. It is for anyone and everyone at all stages of relationship with God.

The Lord constantly visited and spoke to me in amazing ways affirming His message of grace and love. This was either through His word, other ministers or through fellowship with other believers. One Sunday afternoon we held an elders meeting where my fellow elders recommended that I stop teaching the 'things' I was teaching. It is fair to say their concern was valid. The church had stood and grown for many years on half-baked fundamental truths, where righteousness was based on works and not as a free gift. I agreed to stop teaching the gospel of God's grace because it was in confrontation with our doctrine.

The following day, on a Monday morning, my wife received a long text message. Someone interstate had a vivid dream. In that dream, the Lord told them to tell us never to stop teaching that message, not even in one Sunday. This lady was not even in the elders meeting where the Grace message was slaughtered. On another day, when I was down and very discouraged, the Lord spoke to me and said, "what are the names of your children?" To my surprise, He said the names of my children 'is' the message I have for the world. My children's names when interpreted into English mean Grace, Love and Glory. This was unexpected. This brought me to tears. This message of

Jesus is all about rest. **Resting in the finished work of the cross.** But what does this mean?

In this book, I have poured out my life and revealed from the scriptures what it means to live a life of rest. This book will change your life. Don't take my word for it, read it with a bible next to you. Let every statement be qualified by God's Word. To help you fully understand true rest and avoid the many questions that flooded me when I first taught it, I have laid a foundation that will help us see the Bible through the same lenses. This foundation is flooded with biblical proof. If you spend enough time on these foundational truths the rest of the book will make so much sense, you'll start embracing this amazing life so hidden yet so needed and available. While others interpret the Bible by mixing the old and the new, Jesus wants us to view it through the lenses of grace, the New Covenant.

While I love the Lord so much, I have always asked difficult questions. For instance, have you ever been asked questions such as why we don't keep the Sabbath anymore or why others still insist that it be kept since it is in the bible? What about loyalty to a man of God as a pre-condition to God's blessings? It is easy to find yourself imprisoned, living in fear in what is supposed to liberate you. It's all in the bible and seemingly well supported by some verses. They are tough questions that make many people uncomfortable. In many cases, you know very well that something is missing, but you can't pinpoint what exactly. Don't get me wrong here, God has blessed us with His servants to bless us. Our loyalty to them makes their already challenging work way easier.

When our loyalty to them surpasses our loyalty to the scriptures, then that's when problems arise, resulting in many known cases of abuses. This is where this point comes in. probably you hear 'you can't touch the Lord's anointed'. At that point, you realise you are in grief, no freedom at all, dissatisfied about your life yet you can't voice it out because 'you can't question what the man of God has said, for he will curse you'. Probably the man of God is 'so big' and celebrated by many. You're stuck! You become conflicted. What was meant to liberate you has put you into deeper bondage. The challenge is: what do you do. You are probably in this space. You are not alone!

When Jesus came on earth, he had to deal with a well-established religious set up. Your solution should not be anger and aggression. Many of God's servants teach these things out of deep love for God like Saul yet in ignorance. Your solution lies in the scriptures. You may say, 'but how? I have read the bible from cover to cover'. Maybe you even graduated from bible college! I do understand that. While you may have read it from cover to cover, the lenses you used to read will determine the interpretation.

It is in how you interpret the Bible. Whenever the bible is interpreted right, the result is a life of right believing which produces a free, liberated, prosperous, repeated pattern of a life of undeserved favor upon favor. Bible interpretation is not for pastors and prophets only, it is for every child of God who has the Spirit of God in them. In this book, you will see why God's intention is to view and interpret His word through the lenses of His grace and kindness.

Through the lenses of grace, the New Covenant comes to great light, revealing extra-ordinary gems of God's promises to you. The lenses you use to read the bible will affect the way you will interpret it. For example, a child and a mother have two different interpretations of a lolly. A little child sees a lolly as a source of food that needs to be consumed daily for survival. The mother sees it as a treat occasionally, fully knowing that lollies don't have adequate nutritional value. If anyone gives that child lollies daily, the child's perception is that of being loved dearly, yet the mother sees it differently. She doesn't see love from the giver because she knows what lots of lollies can do to you. Why? Because lollies don't make you healthy, they have high sugar content that can affect your teeth permanently. The same activity is seen differently, depending on the lenses used to view it. This is also true with the Bible.

Depending on what lenses you use to look at it you may see the Good News differently from what God intended. God intends that we consider the Scriptures based on the lenses of the New Covenant "which remains forever!" (2 Cor. 3:11b). Depending on how the Bible has been presented to you, sadly it can either be a source of bondage (Rom. 8:15) or a source of liberty (2 Cor. 3:17). The word covenant means a formal agreement that has legal connotations to it. The Strong's dictionary defines it from a Greek word **diatheke**, as 'a disposition, arrangement, of any sort, which one wishes to be valid, the last disposition which one makes of his earthly possessions after his death, a testament or will'. It is common in the bible to see the words covenant, will or testament used interchangeably.

Since the Bible is the true source of our knowledge of God, it must be read with the correct lenses. This cannot be over-emphasised else the ministry that was meant to bring you joy and liberty will seem to bring misery and death (2 Cor. 3:7). So, it is the responsibility of every believer to take heed to the doctrine. The Apostle Paul puts it beautifully in 1 Timothy 4:16 NIV when he says "Watch your life and **doctrine** closely. Persevere in them, because if you do, you will save both yourself and your hearers." The word doctrine is also interpreted teaching in other versions. It is the Greek word didaskalia, whose complete definition according to Strong's dictionary is doctrine, learning, teaching or instruction. So, every believer needs to pay close attention to what they are taught – teaching! Wrong teaching leads to wrong thinking which leads to a wrong life.

As you read this book, I invite you to be open-hearted and diligently search the scriptures so that we can together come to this beautiful conclusion of what God means by "entering His rest". Don't be afraid to interrogate what's written here, for you've been born to freedom. It is this self-determination and asking of genuine questions that unlocks the hidden treasures of wisdom in God's word. I have poured my heart and made myself vulnerable by sharing some of my personal life testimonies with the hope that many people will be helped.

Above all, I have tried to let the scriptures do the talking more than me. Understanding rest has totally transformed my life, marriage, ministry and my professional life. It has brought an unforced rhythm, or regular life pattern of constantly relying on the unearned, undeserved and unmerited accomplishments of Jesus at Calvary. You can love God but remain restless. And that is a great loss. The Apostle Paul says in 1 Timothy 6:6 KJV "But godliness **with** contentment is great gain". Godliness alone is not enough, you need contentment!

You need to enter that place of contentment. That's where true gain or wealth is. The word contentment is taken from the Greek word **autarkeias**, which has an amazing meaning. The New Testament Greek Lexicon defines this word as "a perfect condition of life in which no aid or support is needed; sufficiency of the necessities of life and a mind contented with its lot, contentment". Talk of the rest Christ wants you to enter in, surely it is that perfect place in life in which no aid or support is needed because you are fully supplied, everything you need has already been made available for you. This is true rest. The peace of Jesus dwelling in your heart with all might.

Are you trying harder to live right but still failing? Are evil thoughts still dominating your mind? Do you find yourself negative about almost everything? But you are a Christian and you love God! This book is yours. Are you a pastor or minister trying very hard to grow your church? Or you have a large church but can't take a holiday because of the fear people will leave you? Are you a controlling spouse in fear your partner will cheat on you? You constantly scroll through their phone checking their emails and messages? Are you a student or young person worried about losing friends? Worried about your future? Under pressure to attend a party? Are you employed, in fear of losing your job? Maybe you are trying so hard to get that promotion. Probably you've heard your name mentioned in bad faith and so much is going through your mind. This is your book. If you identify with any of the above, you have to read this as it will transform your life forever. It has already changed mine.

Now, journey with me as I go through the scriptures and get hold of your life through 'resting in Christ'. Lay aside religion and get hold of the scriptures. A lie repeated never makes it the truth. Many years ago, it was believed that the earth was flat. Some still do, but we all now know it is spherical. You may have been taught the contrary all your life, perhaps it is time you open your Bible and your heart and experience Jesus. I encourage you to read this book with an open heart. The Bible refers to the Berean Jews in Acts 17:11 as of "noble character" for they "examined the Scriptures every day to see if what Paul said was true".

In the next chapter, we will look at why we now have to use the lenses of the New Covenant of God's Grace as God's viewpoint to live a fulfilled, victorious life with a regular pattern of God's unmerited favor. This is contrary to the Old Covenant, which was signified by the Law of Moses, which only lasted until Jesus! This has a huge significance in liberating you.

2 | OLD AND NEW COVENANT

Having lived a sinless life, a life of honour and faith; a life of total dependence on the Father, raising the dead and healing the sick, our precious Lord Jesus made an astounding declaration after supper in the Book of Luke 22:20 (NLT). It says that

> "After supper, he took another cup of wine and said, "This cup is the **New Covenant** between God and his people--an agreement **confirmed with my blood**, which is poured out as a sacrifice for you.""

Jesus was taking communion when he told his disciples that there was a "New Covenant between God and his people". The Jews understood that their fathers, through Moses, received a covenant of the Law at Mount Sinai from God. When Jesus mentioned a New Covenant, it was clear that the covenant that they were living in was coming to an end. This New Covenant was "confirmed with my blood", Jesus said. This meant that the commencement of the New Covenant was going to be guaranteed by the shedding of His blood. Without the shedding of Jesus' blood, there is no New Covenant.

Hebrews 9:12 (NLT) affirms this by saying "With his own blood-not the blood of goats and calves-he entered the Most Holy Place once for all time and **secured our redemption forever**." The eternal security of our salvation was purchased using the Blood of Jesus. The payment that ensured the validity of that transaction was the blood of Jesus, the very blood that guarantees our inheritance in the New Covenant of God's grace. Which makes sense why our Lord Jesus said it is an "agreement confirmed with my blood".

The shedding of Jesus' blood 'secured our redemption forever', which is a phenomenal truth, key to how you will live your life. The word redemption means "to return something or pay for it to be returned to your possession". The shedding of the blood of Jesus literally secured and returned us to God, forever. Wow! There is no back and forth here. It was a done deal. This was a complete transaction, and no one could or can reverse it. It was a forever arrangement. If one act of Adam made us lose our position in God (Romans 5:19), surely one act of Jesus could (and it did) secure us back forever.

No matter how well we acted after Adam fell, our actions, good or bad, couldn't undo what Adam had done. It was a done deal. We became sinners until Jesus came, regardless of our good deeds. Jesus, the last Adam, also did something like the first Adam that has made us all righteous forever. He obeyed God. He secured our position in God forever. A position that says we are acceptable, loved based on the obedience of Jesus not ours. So, because of Jesus, we remain forever righteous and that position cannot be changed. This is key because it will determine how you believe. The first Adam disobeyed, and everyone became a sinner. The last Adam obeyed, and everyone who believes becomes righteous forever.

This is wonderful news but pay attention. The New Covenant commenced when Jesus shed His blood and secured our redemption forever. This means that Jesus paid with his life to secure our salvation forever. He gave up His life so that you can gain yours. He died so you can live. He went to hell so you can inherit God's kingdom. He took our curses so we can be blessed forever. Your salvation in Christ is secure forever.

The book of Hebrews shows a comparison of the Old Testament Tabernacle and its sacrifices in comparison to a "greater and more perfect tabernacle that is not made with human hands" with Jesus, its one and only true sacrifice. While the scriptures don't clearly show us on which day, after Jesus was crucified, He presented His blood to the Father, we can safely say that at resurrection the New Covenant commenced. Why at resurrection? Because in the Old order, which was a shadow of reality, if a sacrifice was not accepted the High Priest wouldn't live. The fact that Jesus our High Priest shed his Blood and came out alive and is seated with the Father in Heaven is a reflection that God accepted His sacrifice for our sins, hence the commencement of the new order.

The resurrection of Jesus was a commencement of a New Covenant. Notice, I said the resurrection not the birth. When Jesus was born, His blood was not shed. When

Jesus lived, though He did mighty miracles and wonders, still, His blood was not shed. This means that Jesus did not live during the New Covenant, but He lived to secure it for us on the Cross. This means that the New Covenant life after the resurrection of Jesus is well outlined from the Book of Acts to Revelation. So where does this place the gospels? Matthew, Mark, Luke and John? These are historical books of the life of Jesus. They outline the life of Jesus in an Old Testament setting, with our Lord introducing the New Covenant. These books are like a bridge transitioning the old to the new. These books are significant, and like all other books, need to be studied in context to extract New Covenant truths from them, and learn from the failure, inadequacy or weakness of human effort, legalism and the law of Moses. On the contrary, the New Covenant of God's Grace expresses God's love to man, His goodness like never.

Now this is very key. When I was a young believer, I was told I was perfectly living in the New Covenant since I was speaking in tongues and not keeping the Sabbath. Sadly, churches were separated by whether they worshipped on Saturday (keeping the Sabbath) or on a Sunday, which either way is a myopic view of the Sabbath or the New Covenant. We remained bound in the Old Covenant while professing to live in the New. So, it is good to examine the scriptures to understand what exactly it means to live in the New Covenant as a new creation, **totally at rest on the finished work of the cross**.

What does all this mean? How does it affect my everyday life? We sang good songs with lyrics like "if I live a holy life, shun the wrong and do the right, I know the Lord will make a way for me". Wow, it was a powerful song that made me pray more and love more. It was sung beautifully with passion, but there is a problem. The lyrics of the song were based on the Old testament, affirming the old covenant not what Christ had already done. They say God will only make a "way" for me "if" I do what is right. God's ability to make a way for me is not dependent on what I have done, be it good or not so good. Its dependent on what Jesus has already done, which is perfect in every way and Jesus is that Way anyway. If I were to sing that song today, I would keep the nice beat and change the lyrics to something like "Jesus is my way, now I live a holy life, shun the wrong and do what's right". That changes everything. It means, I am living a holy life, shunning what's wrong and doing what's right because of Jesus! That's the New Covenant talk. And there are many nice songs with lyrics outside the New Covenant.

Ok, lets continue to explore the separation of the covenants. If Matthew, Mark, Luke and John are not the New Testament, where does that put the words spoken by Jesus? How do we read those books? In some Bibles the words spoken by Jesus are in written red. Do we discard them? You see, these are very good questions that should be asked. And they need to be answered by the Bible. Believers who chose not to ask such questions, especially if they don't understand, become the most religious.

I once asked a passionate pastor some of these questions and his response was "Pastor, I don't know, let's just evangelise and win souls into the kingdom". While that sounded nice, it wasn't right. Once the souls are in Christ, then they are brought into bondage by legalism and religion and this pains me. Every book and verse in the Bible should be contextualised to drain the full meaning to us today. The words of Jesus, for example, spoken to the rich young ruler (Mark 10 and Matthew 19), were specific to this young man whose faith in the law was strong. Jesus' advice to this young man was in the context of the young man putting trust in his ability to keep the law. That advice is not the counsel Jesus is giving to all those born of the Spirit. To us, he says, "the just (righteous) shall live by faith".

Ok, now that we appreciate the New Covenant and the position of the gospels, what is the state of the Old Covenant. Where does it begin, where does it end? You are probably saying pastor, I don't need to know about all that, I just want to love God. I get you, and that is part of the problem – not wanting to know. Many believers don't want to know, hence the manipulation in the body of Christ. It is in your interest to understand what you believe. It has a huge bearing on your liberty.

Many believers have come from the bondage of sin to the bondage of man/religion. It ought not to be so. Hebrews 8:13 (NLT) says "When God speaks of a "new" covenant, it means he has made the first one obsolete. It is now **out of date** and will soon disappear." Also, Hebrews 8:7 (NIV) says "For if there had been nothing wrong with that first covenant, no place would have been sought for another." The Word of God does emphasize these covenants. That the Old is now obsolete, out of date and soon to disappear. That sounds too aggressive a language, yet it is in the Bible. It goes on to say, "it had something wrong".

The apostle Paul in 2 Corinthians 3:7 NLT also puts emphasis on the position of the old covenant, using very strong language, he says "The old way, with laws, etched in stone, led to death, though it began with such glory that the people of Israel could not bear to look at Moses' face. For his face shone with the glory of God, even though the brightness was already fading away." You see, he clearly portrays that the Old way, which is the old covenant, which had "laws etched in stone" – referring to commandments written on stone (Exodus 31:18) led to death. He also says even though it was glorious, the glory was fading away, it was disappearing.

The Old Covenant, the Law of Moses, is portrayed with such strong language leading to death, obsolete, out of date and ready to disappear. 2 Corinthians 3:11 (NLT) closes this argument saying: "So if the old way, **which has been replaced**, was glorious, how much more glorious is the new, which remains forever!" – Wow. The Old Testament has been replaced. The Old, obsolete, out of date and ready to disappear covenant of the Law of Moses has been replaced! Hallelujah!

So why would people still want to stick to the Old when the New and better covenant is here? Many believers are at war with anyone wanting to live in the New Covenant of God's Grace. Some of it is out of ignorance. Some of it is simply the fear of losing control over believers who have been established in the Old Covenant of restlessness, fear and rules. While some of it is just demonic. The New Covenant of God's grace brings rest to whosoever believes. The Old Covenant, which commenced at Mount Sinai when Moses received the commandments, ended with Jesus purchasing our redemption forever with His blood at Calvary.

What does this mean? It means that the period before Moses received the Law is NOT the Old Covenant/Testament. What did you just say? You heard right. I'll repeat it. The period before Moses received the law is not in the Old testament. When the Bible talks of the Old covenant it is referring to the period Moses received the Law at Sinai to the time Jesus set us free from the Law when he died and resurrected. Galatians 3:25 (NLT) says "And now that the way of faith has come, **we no longer need the law as our guardian**". Boy, this is so brutal a statement! Did the Bible just say we no longer need the law as our guardian? So, what are we doing trying to manage our lives using the old testament? Check your Bible, this isn't a misquoted verse. We don't need the law as our guardian is what it says. We don't need the Law of Moses to be our guardian, our torch, our navigator. There was now a New way, a better way! The Way of Grace brought by Jesus Christ. The Old Testament Law given to Moses made way for the New Covenant Grace brought by Jesus. It completed what it was meant for and is now of no use, obsolete.

But when did the Law of Moses commence? The way the Bible is generally arranged will make you think that the Old Testament is from Genesis to Malachi and the New Testament is from Matthew to Revelation. But that is not correct. What? Yes, it's not. Look at it this way. A marriage covenant is considered valid the day the certificate is signed. You may have been in a love relationship for years, had kids and purchased property but that doesn't legally count as marriage. You can scream all the way that you have been together and show evidence of doing things together but still, it doesn't count as a marriage covenant in the true biblical sense of marriage, not cohabiting. When you separate with that person you are never called a divorcee because the rules that go with the marriage covenant don't apply to you. Most people would simply say 'I'm no longer with my partner' because legally, they were not married, but just living together. Moses had to say this in Deut. 5:2-3 NLT, when he was addressing the children of Israel, I quote:

"2 The Lord our God made a covenant **with us** at Mount Sinai. 3 The Lord **did not** make this covenant with our ancestors, **but with all of us** who are alive today."

Wow, see that? Here Moses clearly excluded Abraham, Isaac and Jacob from the Old Covenant of the Law because "The Lord did not make" the covenant with them. By ancestors, he was referring to all those who lived before them. By "us" he was referring to himself and all those that left Egypt. This is pivotal. This is the reason why when you read the scriptures you will notice that it is never recorded that Abraham, Isaac and Jacob kept the Law or followed certain requirements of the Law. Reason being the Law had not yet been given.

The Old Covenant Law was given to Moses and the children of Israel at Mount Sinai and they would live under the requirements of that covenant until a New Covenant was introduced, making the old one obsolete. Understanding this bit will change your life forever. It will simplify a lot of things we do as believers and will set you free from many rituals of the old covenant. And remember, being in a modern church, with lights and good music doesn't necessarily mean it is a new testament church. What is taught is what determines whether that gathering is teaching Christ or Moses. As a believer, you should be able to discern what is right and what is wrong regardless of who it comes from. Anyway, what you do with what you hear will affect the quality of your life not of the person who said it to you.

Ok, so where does that place the period before Moses received the Law in terms of covenants? From the beginning, God has always been loving and gracious to man. He does not change. When man sinned, God remained the same. When man demanded the Law, God remained the same. When man demanded a king, God remained the same, He does not change. The writer of Galatians, the apostle Paul, answers the question of the period before Moses received the Law.

Galatians 3:17-18NIV "17What I mean is this: The law, introduced 430 years later, **does not set aside the covenant previously established by God** and thus do away with the **promise**. 18For **if** the inheritance depends on the law, then it no longer depends on the promise; but God **in his grace** gave it to Abraham through a promise.

This is too good. The apostle Paul reminds us that God "in His Grace" made a promise to Abraham – which was actually a "covenant previously established by God". God's promise to Abraham was another covenant! Stay with me. He continues and says that the entrance of the Law of Moses did not annul that promise. Verse 16 says: "The promises were spoken to Abraham and his seed…which is Christ". This is wonderful! You see; the Abrahamic covenant was God's ideal plan for man until they requested for the Law. And that covenant of promise was a covenant of God's grace.

The Abrahamic covenant, signified by the circumcision on the 8th day of every male, has all the tenets of a Grace covenant of the New Testament. God was the guarantor of that covenant, not Abraham. We see God dealing with Abraham, Isaac and Jacob and eventually the children of Israel by grace until they reached Mt Sinai when they chose the law by their constant grumbling. So, from Abraham to Mount Sinai, the covenant of the promise was in force, and it was a grace-based covenant. This did not cease at Mount Sinai when the law came because "the law did not annul the promise".

Before Abraham, we do not see any specific covenant that God cut with man, yet we still find God overly gracious. He deals with man according to grace right from the beginning. The period from creation to the giving of the promise to Abraham is "the beginning". From Abraham to Moses at Mount Sinai, it is the promise (though it did not cease when the law arrived). From Sinai to the death of Jesus was "the Law" and from the resurrection of Christ to date, we're in "Grace".

The way we believe will affect the way we live. During the law, they constantly lived with the hope that God will bless them if they do good. That was right then, under the law covenant. But after the arrival of the New Covenant, signatured by the blood of Jesus, we constantly live in this assurance that God loves us and has already blessed us with all spiritual blessings in the heavenly realms. We are secure. If you live your Christian life based on the old, you will constantly be trying to appease God by your effort to get him to do what he already did through Jesus on the cross.

3 | Understanding the New Covenant

I hope the previous chapter has shed some understanding in separating the covenants. In this chapter let's explore the covenant we live in and see how this precious life of unforced rhythms of grace can be lived. This life of perpetual rest in Christ Jesus. This life of freedom and lightness. For many years I lived a life of obligation. I was obliged to pray, fast, serve, give, preach and do so many other things because of the notion that, if I didn't do so God wouldn't bless me as much. Worse still, I thought he would punish me for being disobedient to Him. I would fast once a week, pray at a certain time at night in fear of demonic attacks.

Reading the book "dangerous prayers" did not make things easier as it made me more conscious of evil instead of good. You see, there was this huge compulsion to do things a certain way, in case I got bad luck. It was so terrible that at the beginning of every year we were obligated to fast for many days so that either the devil doesn't attack us that year or God blesses us. Prayer and fasting are wonderful disciplines of Christianity, and I've written about restful prayer later in this book, but they lose the wonder when done in fear or bondage. I was so insecure, so were many of those around me. While all those things are good Christian principles, I was not doing them out of rest, but out of fear. Fear was the motivation, not love.

Fasting and prayer has some of the most amazing benefits to a believer, but only when done with the right motive and understanding. of what God expects of us as Christians. While I accepted that Jesus delivered me more than 2,000 years ago when He died on the cross, it would seem by my beliefs that I didn't actually accept that he completed his work. In that case, I sought further deliverance to complete what Jesus had already done. Sounds familiar? There are many people still bound by this. I am absolutely free, and all this is in the past.

The difference between the Old and the New Covenants is that the Old is obligation driven, while the New is love-driven. Same things appear in both the Old and New, for example, prayer and giving. In the New we pray and give because of the love nature that God put in us; it's our nature to do so. Inspiringly effortless!

Since it is our nature, the New Covenant is a covenant that allows us to live with a sense and reality of rest. No self-effort. Isn't that amazing news? Ok, look at this example. Do you struggle to be a human being? I mean living as a human compared to living like an animal e.g. a dog or cat. Definitely not, why? Because you have human nature in you. So, you are at rest because that's your nature.

You don't sleep hoping that you'll wake up with your brains in your head. It doesn't even cross your mind because you are human, and your brains are intact in your skull. You function totally at rest. As a new creation in Christ, we are secure with the nature that makes us live victoriously, at rest in Him.

One key element of the New Covenant of God's Grace is rest. It is God's will for man, right from the beginning. When God created the heavens and the earth, he packaged all things that man needed – light, animals, trees, plants, air, water and every other thing we see today. On the sixth day, God made man – with everything he needed already provided for him. You see, man was never meant to be stressed, he was meant to be at rest. Amazingly, God declared the following day after creating man a Sabbath rest. It was the seventh day; a day God had completed everything he needed to do. You see, man's first day of existence was to rest in God's finished work. It has always been God's plan; for man to be at rest, not to be weary and heavy-laden. Not to be stressed. God's will for man is not to stress, but live in peace, rest and goodness of constant supply. "Look at the birds of the air, for they neither sow nor reap nor gather into barns; yet your heavenly Father feeds them. Are you not of more value than they?" (Matthew 6:26-27).

Today we live in the Grace Covenant. Life under God's Grace is a life of triumph over sin. It's a life of overcoming. It's a life of being more than conquerors because of what our Lord Jesus has already done for you and me. Romans 5:17 NLT says "For the sin of this one man, Adam, caused death to rule over many. But even greater is God's wonderful grace and his gift of righteousness, for all who receive it will live in triumph over sin and death through this one man, Jesus Christ." So, in grace, receiving grace and the gift of righteousness is the key to triumph over sin. A life of sin is a life of restlessness. A life without sin is a life overflowing with God's Rest.

2 Cor. 5:17NIV says "Therefore, if anyone is in Christ, the new creation has come: The old has gone, the new is here!" A new creation life is lived in the New Covenant, which is guaranteed by the blood of Jesus. True success and prosperity are experienced when believers live within the confines of the New Covenant. Prophet Jeremiah, under the inspiration of God's Spirit, prophesied about this coming New Covenant. What I love about this prophecy is that it also relates to the Old Covenant, and about 600years before Jesus was born.

Jeremiah 31:31-33 NLT

31"The day is coming," says the Lord, "when I will make a **New Covenant** with the people of Israel and Judah. **32This covenant will not be like the one I made with their ancestors** when I took them by the hand and brought them out of the land of Egypt. They broke that covenant, though I loved them as a husband loves his wife," says the Lord. 33"But this is the **New Covenant** I will make with the people of Israel on that day," says the Lord. "I will put my instructions deep within them, and I will write them on their hearts. I will be their God, and they will be my people.

You see, the New Covenant is not a fabrication by a few crazy preachers. It was God's plan even during the law of Moses. God has always wanted human beings to live under His grace, the New Covenant. Notice, God says He "will make a New Covenant". It's not man who made the New Covenant. God is the author of the New Covenant. We are beneficiaries of this covenant. It was never in God's will for us to operate under the law, never. The New Living Translation puts it clearly in Galatians 3:19 by saying "Why, then, was the law given? It was given alongside the promise **to show people their sins**. But the law was designed to last only until the coming of the child who was promised. God gave his law through angels to Moses, who was the mediator between God and the people."

The purpose of the Law was never to make us righteous. If it had the power to make us right before God, then Jesus didn't need to come. The purpose of the law was "to show us our sins" and more-so that we need a Saviour. It was never meant to be permanent; it was temporary. So, a child of God, born again, a new creation, lives their life using the lenses of the New Testament, not the old testament. This is a game-changer. Prayer in the Old is different from prayer in the New. In the Old prayer was an attempt to get God to do what Jesus eventually did and completed on the cross. In the New, prayer is appropriating what Jesus has already done by dying for us on that cross. In the Old, they approached God in fear while we now approach God in joy and gladness because of what Jesus has done for us. They also lived right through their own power and strength. But we live right because Jesus bestowed unto us the nature that allows us to live right by default – the gift of righteousness.

My friend, knowing your identity as a new creation believer in the New Covenant has the power to revolutionise your life. I'll take this time to ask you a question. If you are a believer, is your life governed by the New Covenant or you are still stuck in the old, fading, death-bringing covenant of the law? Ok, I can hear someone saying; "I speak in tongues", "I keep the Sabbath" and "in our church, we prophesy" and there are many examples. Ok, that's fine, but are you righteous? What do you need to do to be righteous? Again, I can hear some answers like "I need to confess to a priest", "I need to do all the right things and not sin", etc. You see, I can ask a whole lot of questions. What I'm driving at is that if you have answered as above you are probably still stuck in the Old Covenant. Jesus purchased righteousness for us when He died on the cross. It is now a free gift of God. (Rom. 5:17)

Understanding the New Covenant is foundational to your faith and liberty in Christ "…for you no longer live under the requirements of the law. Instead, you live under the freedom of God's grace" (Romans 6:14NLT). Instead of putting effort into trying to understand "the requirements of the law", it is essential that you invest time trying to understand "living under the freedom of God's Grace". Many people argue and say we still need the law to keep us under check. My question is, do you think God is not smart enough to declare that grace is the appropriate solution, if the law is? Of course, the wisdom of man is foolishness to God. Man thinks the rules and regulations; the requirements of the law can do a good job in producing right living, yet God rejected that model. Friends, the freedom of God's grace is the answer to every problem brought by sin.

A lot of biblical subjects such as giving, prayer, deliverance, sacrifices, etc. become problematic without an understanding of the foundation of the New Covenant. There is a church that believes that to be born again you have to pray a lot, fast until you see an angel which then confirms that you have been saved. Honestly? Where do we find such things in scripture? It sounds passionate and quite devotional but that's not the way God intended in the New Covenant. I once asked believers when I was ministering at a certain church that at what point do you know you have been forgiven when you ask for forgiveness of your sins from God. The responses were many blanks until someone said; "you feel it". Wow, I said. What about you don't feel anything for days, and weeks? Condemnation sets in. You feel dirty, unaccepted by God and you don't feel confident to approach the Father.

In the New Covenant, God forgave us all our sins when Jesus died and resurrected. Every sin, past, present and future has been paid for, which means you have been forgiven already. But pastor Sbanga, what do you mean? If I sin, already God has forgiven me? Yes, that's the good news. It's too good to be true hey? You only need to accept His forgiveness. You have to receive and live under that wonderful covering of His grace. I'm not going to exhaust all in here, but you get the idea. It is key to understand the foundations of the New Covenant as God intended.

Grace is a wonderful, glorious life of God's goodness, free from the dominion of sin and oppression. It is a fulfilling life of living without sin effortlessly, not because we are trying hard to but because God has *"put his instructions deep within us," (Jer 31:33NLT)* – his nature of righteousness. We don't put effort not to sin. It's our nature not to. A bird never puts an effort to fly, it just flies. Why, it's the nature of birds to fly. Try to jump over a tall building hoping to fly, we'll probably attend your funeral. Why? It is not your nature to fly. You can try very hard to fly like a bird, but you probably won't go far. The best we can do is design technology that can fly us. For example, an aeroplane but it's also limited. On the other hand, the creator embedded in the human design abilities that birds of the air can't do. So, in the New Covenant, God has given us His nature, the nature of righteousness. It is that nature that modifies our behaviour supernaturally. Romans 5:17 says we need to "receive" this gift of righteousness and abundance of grace so that we can live a life of triumph over sin. Reigning over sin is reigning in life.

Finally, since the New Covenant is confirmed by Jesus' blood then it means it commences after the resurrection of Christ – when the grave, sting of death and the power of sin was defeated. Since the resurrection of Christ is mentioned in Matthew 28, Mark 16, Luke 24 and John 20, where does this place these books seeing the resurrection happens on their last chapters (except John, which is in second of the last chapter)? Good question. These four books are historical books chronicling the life of Jesus on earth. They are not the New Covenant.

The life of Jesus is portrayed in the Old Testament setting in these four books. Jesus introduces the New Covenant of grace while at the same time he confronts the Pharisees on their confidence in the law. Some people have argued, out of a good heart, that the words said by Jesus (in some Bibles written in red) should be followed as they are. But remember that the whole Bible is "God-breathed" according to 2 Tim. 3:16. So instead of picky choosing what Jesus said we may as well say every verse should be followed as it is because God's breath is upon every verse. That is not helpful. Every verse should be interpreted in its context using the lenses of the New Covenant, extracting the truths for our use today.

This changed my life, my ministry! I desire that the same happens as you continue to read through this book. The New Covenant life will bring rest to your soul. When fully understood and embraced you will start experiencing extra-ordinary quiet in your life. Not that there are no challenges and issues, but in the midst of those you are at peace. Jesus portrayed a wonderful expression of rest while he was on earth, He lived a new creation life.

4 | JESUS OUR REST

The word panic never existed in the vocabulary of Jesus. Jesus never reacted to situations, he was always at peace, at rest. For a start, He was rested about His relationship with the Father. Listen to the intimacy and restfulness of the prayer He made in John 17:21. He spoke about the Father with so much fondness, security and restfulness. He didn't expect that the Father would abandon Him anytime. He knew He was on His side all the time. This is the quality God intends for all His children. To be secure and restful and be fond and close to Him with no expectation of being abandoned. You see in the New Covenant, that is the life that has been given to us through Jesus Christ. Jesus prayed saying, "I pray that they will all be one, *just as you and I are one--as you are in me, Father, and I am in you*. And may they be in us so that the world will believe you sent me."

Jesus spoke to the Father as if He was next to Him. It was an intimate conversation. Look at that statement, *"just as you and I are one--as you are in me, Father, and I am in you"*. Jesus knew that He was at peace with the Father. He didn't question it. He knew that He was loved, protected and cared for. He didn't stress. He further went on to say, "as you are in me, Father, and I am in you". Such a language or description of closeness to the father was difficult to understand to the extent that at some stage Phillip had to say "Lord, show us the Father and that will be enough for us." (John 14:8) You see, they heard so much about the Father they wanted to finally see Him. Jesus loved the Father so much. Spoke about Him all the time, displayed satisfaction and security in Him! Boy, He was at rest in Him.

I sent my children for an eleven-day holiday visiting my sister in Darwin, NT, Australia. When they came back home in Brisbane, they kept saying how much they missed us, love us, and how there is no place like home. I was thinking really, my sister spoiled you, took you to places and you had heaps of fun. When I looked into their eyes, they welled with so much love and affection, a connection that melts your heart away. They were in love with us their parents. My own experience makes me understand how intimate Jesus is to the Father. They are together, He is in Him and vice versa. What manner of love is that?

You see, we witness Jesus' state of rest throughout his life. One day, in Mark 4, at night, after a day of ministry He decided to travel to the other side of the lake in a boat. As they travelled, soon a fierce storm came up. High waves were breaking into the boat, and it began to fill with water. Now this is a practical situation where things have gone wrong and their lives were at stake. Look at verse 38, it says "Jesus was **sleeping** at the back of the boat with **his head on a cushion**. The disciples woke him up, shouting,

"Teacher, don't you care that we're going to drown?" Really? How could He sleep when they were in such danger? Exactly! God wants us to be at rest regardless of what is really happening around us. Jesus had his head on a cushion. He was at rest. Why? He knew the father was in Him, and the Father cannot drown. He was protected, at peace at rest. He knew His authority. His disciples didn't, they were in a state of unrest, fear. They panicked, came running to where Jesus was, shouting at Him.

Unrest will cause you to blame others for things they are not responsible for. They blamed Jesus as if he was meant to do something. Jesus, from a position of rest, brought quiet to a raging storm, a storm of a hurricane proportion! Every storm around you will respond to your state of rest. Rest displays that you are content and have everything you need for this life. Jesus quietened the storm and "it was perfectly calm". When you have rest in you, you bring perfect calm to every raging disorder around you.

Marriages that are in turmoil will miraculously be healed because of the rest resident in you. Unrest is a result of unbelief and worsens already bad situations. The disciples couldn't believe that they would survive based on the fierceness of the storm. Jesus was enraged at that. He didn't blame the storm, no! He quietened the storm and said to the disciples "Why are you afraid? Do you still have no faith?". He was amazed at their lack of faith – their unbelief. The issue is not sickness, poverty, debt or even joblessness. As long as we live on this fallen earth, these will always be there. The issue is your failure to be at rest in recognition that Jesus has given you all you need to weather any storm.

Friends, God is interested to have you live a perpetual life of rest. The exciting thing is that He has already done it for you, you just need to receive it and have it. He is above sickness, lack, failure and cannot be contained by time. When Lazarus died, his sisters were distraught. More-so they had told Jesus while there was still time when he was alive. When Jesus arrived four days later, He was calm, collected, at peace. He did not weep because He was overwhelmed by the death of Lazarus, no. Initially, he had declared that his sickness would not end in death, but Lazarus was now dead.

When Martha came to him, Jesus still declared that 'he will live again'. Jesus wept because He saw them weeping. He didn't weep because He could have avoided Lazarus' death, no. He felt their grief. He is the resurrection and the life. He loved them so much He experienced their grief. Friends, that's exactly how much God loves you. He feels your grief, your pain and knows your needs before you even ask Him. That's why He went about doing good, healing the sick and opening blind eyes. Jesus is overflowing in love and mercy. He loves you so much He can count the number of your hairs. He wants you to share the same life He has, a life full and overflowing with faith, a life of rest.

I was impressed by a boxing fight that took place in August of 2017 between Floyd Mayweather and Conor McGregor. Mayweather was already an undisputed champion while McGregor was looking at bringing a huge international boxing upset. My impression was what McGregor said concerning his opponent. And the beauty with the internet is that you can look it up. He said after losing the match, I quote: "He's composed, he's not that fast, he's not that powerful, but boy is he composed in there,". Rest gives you composure. The synonyms of the word composure include being "calm, collected, cool, controlled, self-controlled, serene, tranquil, relaxed, at ease, self-possessed, unruffled, unperturbed, unflustered, undisturbed, unmoved, unbothered, untroubled and unagitated". You see, Conor was surprised how his opponent was not "as fast" or "as powerful", probably because that's what is expected of a champion, at least in boxing. I believe Mayweather knew who he was, what he was capable of, and regardless of hard punches from his opponent, his greatest weapon was to focus on who he was and his own ability. My friend, that is called rest.

Remaining composed, calm, unperturbed, untroubled, unmoved, unagitated in the midst of the worst because you know that Jesus took care of it more than 2,000 years ago is called rest. Isaiah 26:3NLT says "You will keep in *perfect peace* all who trust in you, all whose thoughts are fixed on you!" It is God who will keep you in that perfect peace, not yourself! Your duty is to keep your "thoughts" fixed on Jesus – Christ Consciousness. That phrase perfect peace is in Hebrew "shalom-shalom", and the Strong's dictionary defines that as "safe, well, happy, friendly, health, prosperity, peace". Wow! This is too good. And the phrase is actually used as a noun, which means it refers to "a person, a thing or a place". Isaiah 9:6 refers to Jesus as the Prince of peace. It all points to Jesus! He is our perfect peace. Our shalom shalom, our rest!

It doesn't stop there. This definition of 'shalom-shalom' is synonymous with the definition of the word salvation, Sozo in Greek, which means "to save, deliver or protect, heal, preserve, do well, be made whole" and Jesus is our Saviour! 2 Peter 3:18NIV says "But grow in the grace and knowledge of our Lord and *Saviour* Jesus Christ. To him be glory both now and forever! Amen." He is our life, our rest our perfect peace – shalom-shalom, hallelujah! Jesus is the epitome of rest, of your peace.

You see, resting in God doesn't mean the absence of danger or trouble. No. it means remaining calm in spite of any impending trouble and persecution. It also means you don't blame others. You stand on the fact that God loves you, cares and will never leave nor forsake you. Your faith remains firm, strong and totally immovable. In fact, it never crosses your mind that God has abandoned you.

There was a time when my wife and I experienced rejection, abandonment and humiliation. We had diligently served many people for many years, but the same people walked away when we needed them most. Others walked away with a kiss, while others walked away cursing and swearing. We had helped many financially, protected some from physical danger, stood guard to defend crumbling marriages. When we made ourselves vulnerable, their lives and families prospered. Sadly, when it mattered most, when we needed them most, they walked away.

The pain was unbearable. Most of the pain was not in those that had attacked us, but the experience of those we had stood with for many years, who walked away when we needed them most. Does this sound familiar? I had no income. In the midst of that time we held onto one truth, that God would never leave us nor forsake us (Hebrews 13:5 and Deuteronomy 13:5). That truth was so real, so powerful. In the midst of all that, barely a month after these things, I remember one afternoon, during a photoshoot at my house, I got a phone call, "your three children have been involved in a car accident, the car is a right off". I just sat there motionless. I didn't know how to feel. I then walked upstairs, into my bedroom and shed a few tears. In my mind the devil kept saying "which one of them is dead? You see, God has abandoned you". It was a storm, of a hurricane proportion. I had lost my friends, income and now a possibility of losing my children! I broke the news to my wife. She was unusually calm.

I had anticipated that she would scream or at least cry but she didn't. Many questions of unrest tried to race in my mind. What if they were dead? What if they were badly injured? A wonderful godly lady, sister Heather, who was doing my wife's makeup during the photoshoot kindly drove us to the scene. I was praying in tongues all the way. That helped a lot. When we arrived, from a distance there were about six ambulances, police cars and private cars. A crowd of onlookers had gathered to see what was happening. On the far end, was my Ford Territory. The back of the car was crushed badly and instantly I knew my little daughter was sitting on that spot.

At that time, both of us had this unusual peace- really amazing. We knew God had us in the palm of His hand. Our lives were secure. Guess what, miraculously all our children were not badly hurt. The other two had no injuries at all, while my little girl had a light cut in the head, nothing serious. When I checked on the brother who was driving my kids, he was full of condemnation, but my heart was so overflowing of God's peace. The Holy Spirit nudged me not to ask him to pay excess of $1,800.00 towards insurance, though he was liable to. Though I didn't have the money, no income, I was so much at peace and at rest. This can only be the love of God for us. It seemed there was a great power at work in us, upholding us, cheering us on.

You may have encountered similar situations in your life. As you reflect on those circumstances, I pray that you start experiencing such manner of rest. A place of no condemnation, no hatred, but supernatural peace and grace without self-effort. Only God's effort. God's rest doesn't mean living in denial. A person living in denial is usually in constant grief and is using their effort not to appear cracking under pressure. On the contrary, a person living in rest is different. They know something bad happened or is happening, but they are so calm and peaceful and cannot pinpoint the source of their tranquil apart from God. That is the rest that God brings. It is supernatural. It is comforting to know that He gives it to whosoever desires. Just like oxygen is available to everyone to live on through breathing because God has supplied an overabundance of it; if you choose not to breathe it, you'll die.

God's rest is available, freely made available by His Grace. If you don't receive it, you'll labour in vain. Two years after this hurricane on our lives, our progress has been phenomenal if not miraculous. Jesus Christ is our rest. He lived a life of complete rest to the point of death, even death on the cross. That same Jesus now lives in you. No, you did not get that, I said He now lives in you. That truth is transformational. Galatians 2:20NIV says, "I have been crucified with Christ and I no longer live, but **Christ lives in me**. The life I now live in the body, I live by faith in the Son of God, who loved me and gave himself for me." Romans 8:10NLT goes further to seal this amazing grace fact by saying "And **Christ lives within you**, so even though your body will die because of sin, the Spirit gives you life because you have been made right with God." Do you notice something on both verses? The emphasis of "lives". That word is present continuous tense. Which means it's something that is happening right now and will continue to. You literally believe it to experience it.

Colossians 1:27NIV also highlights this glorious gift of God's grace by saying "to whom God has chosen to make known among the Gentiles the glorious riches of this mystery, which is **Christ in you**, the hope of glory." This is infectious, it is lovely! The presence of Jesus in you is referred to as "glorious riches". If the Bible describes it this way there's gonna be something about it, and there is. You see, Jesus, full of grace and truth (John 1:14), totally at rest has made His residence in you and is alive. What does that mean? It means you have the rest of Jesus in you. Jesus Christ is your rest, He is my rest, He is our rest.

This tells us that we can sleep in a storm just like Jesus did. When Jesus was hanging on the cross, in pain and agony, rejected by man, he was in a state of calm, peace and divine unexpected rest. 1 Peter 2:23NLT describes this wonderfully. It says "He did not retaliate when he was insulted, nor threaten revenge when he suffered. He left his case in the hands of God, who always judges fairly." Wow! That's Jesus, the prince of peace. Instead, He cried out and said "Father, forgive them, for they do not know what they are doing" (Luke 23:34). In Acts 7:60 Stephen, after being stoned for his testimony about Jesus, facing imminent death, out of the abundance of his heart said "...Lord, do not hold this sin against them...". Do you notice that he used similar words like Jesus? Aha, you get it. It wasn't him talking. It was "Christ living in him" talking. No normal human being can speak like that in that situation. True rest, friends, is when Jesus lives freely in our lives. He is our rest. Without Him there is no rest. Grace allows Christ to bring rest to our emotions, completely to our being. That is life brothers and sisters. The panic and stress that believers go through when trouble affects them is inconsistent with who they are, totally inconsistent with the new divine nature that Christ has put in us.

Ok, you might say pastor you don't understand, my situation is worse I feel overwhelmed; that's why I'm stressed. You're not being sensitive pastor. Please pray for me or do something. Can't God do something? You know, I fully understand your frustration, but only one person can do something about it. And that happens to be you. The trouble may not go away instantly as the scriptures teach in

John 16:33NIV when Jesus said "I have told you these things, so that **in me you may have peace**. In this world, you will have trouble. But take heart! **I have overcome the world**." Two references are given here, either to be "In Me", Jesus says or "In the world". He says, "in Me" you will "have peace", but "in this world" you will find "trouble". Wow! You can choose, to be in Christ or in the world. To walk in peace or in trouble or turmoil. You need to believe what Jesus says in the latter part of that verse, that "He has overcome the world", so be at peace, be at rest. What you need is to trust Jesus, and rest in Him amid that storm. Will you be embarrassed? That's ok, it's better to be embarrassed with Jesus than to be glorified without him. That's a life given totally to Him. Let Christ be your rest. He wants to help you so badly, that's why He lives in you. Give Him room and let Him live this life for you. There is no reason why you should harbour anger and jealousies. Just overflow in forgiveness and celebrate other people's successes. That's who you are!

And by the way, when my children were involved in that car crash, it was barely a month after we had experienced massive rejection, vilification and loss. It was like the evil day had come to us (Ephesians 6:13). On the ground, there was nothing pretty to glory about except Christ in us, the only hope of Glory. You can do it too. Let Jesus live this life for you. We managed to stand, and are still standing now, almost five years after that dark cloud in our lives. And the Lord has given us new friends, new income, a new life and we are happier, even more, resting in His goodness. The source of unrest in an unbeliever is the absence of Jesus in them. They need to be born again and Christ will come in them to give them a new life (2 Cor. 5:17). On the other hand, the source of unrest in believers is unbelief. Jesus is in them, but they don't believe what He teaches them, to truly give them rest in their souls. In the next chapter, I explain this even further.

5 | Unrest and Unbelief

When Jesus resurrected in great victory and triumph, He designed New Covenant life, grace life or commonly Christianity to be very simple and fulfilling such that it takes a theological professor to complicate it. Transitioning from the Old Testament of rules and sacrifices, the New was what everyone longed for. You see, oppressive Christianity thrives on human effort where you feel you must do something to achieve what Christ has already achieved. For example, the Greek word 'Sōzo', generally translated save in English includes deliverance as part of its wide definition.

Ephesians 2:8NIV says that by grace we have been saved *(includes deliverance)* through faith and this is not from yourselves, it is the gift of God. Let's zero this verse on deliverance, one of the definitions of sōzo. It would partly say 'by grace you *have been delivered* through faith…' in italics it says you have been delivered – that's past tense. I have a question for you, do you believe that statement? That you have been delivered already? If you answered yes, then I'll ask another question: why are Christians still pursuing further deliverance? Why are deliverance ministries thriving all over the world? Probably your answer would be, pastor you don't understand. You're right, I don't understand why you would believe that you are delivered and not believe it the same time. It's a special condition that prevented the children of Israel from inheriting the promised land, it is called unbelief. Unbelief is deadly.

Some will say you've never been to Africa or India where witchcraft is real and being born again is not enough. Really? Is this not making the grace of God of no effect according to Galatians 2:21? If the grace of God is of no effect and meaningless then Ephesians 2:8 cannot be true, then we need other means of getting what Jesus declared as finished on the cross. One of those things declared as finished was deliverance. God forbid! Unbelief confronts the validity of God's word. Because of unbelief, believers will continue seeking to deliver other Christians from many things such as generational curses, bad luck etc. and yet Jesus dealt with that once and for all, declaring the devil forever defeated. It shows that many religious people do not trust the grace of God to give them power over sin. On the other hand, they trust their own hard work! Let me explain a bit about God's grace.

Grace is Jesus Christ himself. You can't get grace and not have Jesus, neither can you get Jesus and not get grace. It's like being in the water and not getting wet. If you get into the water, you'll be wet. You can't separate wetness with water. Water wets! Jesus graces! In John 1:14 NIV the Bible says "The Word became flesh and made **his** dwelling among us. We have seen **his** glory, the glory of the one and only Son, who came from the Father*,* **full of grace and truth**." When Jesus came, in Him, in His capacity of who

He was and still is, was grace. Unmerited, unearned and undeserved favour. He was 100% full of grace. The coming of Jesus was the coming of Grace. You can't separate those two. Receiving Jesus and refusing the grace He provides is like drinking water and refusing to be quenched of your thirst. Beloved, God's grace is all you need to live in this life. Until you accept that fact, you're on your own.

I can hear someone saying pastor Sbanga, what about truth? Yes; you are right. Jesus was full of truth; in fact, He is truth. He declared this in John 14:6 when He said "… I am the way and the truth and the life…" You see if Jesus is Truth, and Jesus is Grace, and Jesus came full of both Truth and Grace, it tells you that if you get Jesus you get both grace and truth, isn't it? It tells you more. It tells you that the Truth about Jesus is revealed in God's Grace. And the Grace of God reveals Truth about God. You can't separate grace and truth. It's two sides representing the same coin. Jesus is best revealed in the revelation of God's grace to mankind in the fullness of truth.

Friends, the outcome of living in grace negates the need for self-effort in dealing with sin and living everyday life. You see, many people believe what I have just said above, but the problem is they don't believe it. That sounds like an oxymoron hey. Believing but yet not believing. One day a father with a sick child was caught in this and he said to Jesus "I do believe; help me overcome my unbelief!" (Mark 9:24). You can be an unbelieving believer. Ok, let's have a look at more scripture.

Did you know that Jesus was incensed at some towns, Bethsaida and Chorazin, that had received miracles yet remained in ***unbelief!*** Just like today's believer who receives the miracle of 'Christ living in them' yet remain in unbelief. He declared that if the same miracles were performed in Sodom, it would have been saved. You see Sodom was this very sinful city while Bethsaida and Chorazin were very unbelieving cities. Jesus compares unbelief and sinfulness. This is like comparing two devils. Jesus insinuates that a sinful city that goes on to believe is far better than a city with unbelief. Where there is unbelief, nothing happens. Everything is viewed with suspicion. It can't be God. If it is God, why now, there could be a catch. Unbelief is bad. Spirit-filled born-again believers can walk in unbelief. Unbelief is a very bad state of ***unrest*** – Unbelief and Un-Rest is a declaration of no trust in God – It's an issue of trust. It boils down to trust issues. Grace brings rest. Let's have a look at what Jesus said after rebuking Bethsaida and Chorazin:

Matthew 11:25-26 NIV "At that time Jesus said, I praise you, Father, Lord of heaven and earth, because you have hidden these things from the wise and learned and revealed them to **little children.** 26 Yes, Father, for this is what you were pleased to do."

The phrase little children used in this verse is the Greek word "**nephios**" which, according to Thayer's Dictionary means infants, a minor, a little child, untaught and unskilled. The context of this verse doesn't mean that God favours those who are unskilled, no ways. On the contrary, it is a powerful thing to be appropriately informed and walk in wisdom and skill. I encourage my children to learn every musical instrument, play sports, study and just work hard. It's good to be smart and intelligent. Anyway, we have the mind of Christ, so it pleases the Lord when His children excel in various areas of skill. But in this verse, the context was the wisdom and knowledge of the Pharisees about the Father. Their view of the Father was worldly. Their knowledge, wisdom and skill were mature, only through the systems and viewpoint of the world, not the Word. The infants, unskilled and untaught in this context refers to those who have not mastered the art of viewing the Father through the eyes of a sinful world and/or religion. Their viewpoint unschooled in the world, totally unskilful in the worldly systems. The apostle John also says in 1 John 4:5 NIV "They are from the world and therefore speak *from the viewpoint* of the world, and the world listens to them".

Jesus explains that God the Father has hidden the revelation of the Father from those who have a viewpoint of the world, but has revealed those things to "minors" that is, those who have appropriated the grace of God in their lives, those who are born of God, who see all things through God's viewpoint, the viewpoint of the Word. Those are the ones who are at rest in God. In Verse 27 of Mathew 11, Jesus continues and says "**All things** have been committed to me by my Father. No one knows the Son except the Father, and no one knows the Father except the Son and those to whom the Son **chooses to reveal him**." The son, Jesus, chooses to reveal to "those who are at rest in Him" Those at rest in Him are those who have shifted from unbelief to belief, from the world's viewpoint to God's viewpoint. You see, rest is trusting the viewpoint of the Bible through God's eyes of grace concerning your life.

God wants you to be at rest in Him. To walk away from unbelief and step into believing. To trust every aspect of God's word. He wants you to trust Him deal with sin, healing your disease, supplying your needs, etc. Trust is pivotal. Read it and believe it. As a man believes so is he. We believe what we think about (Prov. 23:7). And our thoughts are flooded with what has been given room to our minds. And we choose what we want to give room to our minds. I suggest you choose the Word today. Chose rest. Let the Word of God's Grace dwell richly in your mind. It will shape your thinking, then your believing and eventually your life. Unbelief is embracing the wrong sources of knowledge. Belief is embracing Jesus' source of knowledge, and that knowledge is powered by God's grace, hallelujah! Oh, how I wish you can live this life of liberty in Christ, provided by God's grace.

Unbelief works this way. I'll give an example. Suppose my wife believes and always confesses that I can fix leaking taps at home. You ask her many times and probably she even boasts about it. Yet when a tap leaks, she insists we get a plumber to fix it. That is unbelief. She believes in my ability to fix the tap, but she doesn't believe I can do it when the tap starts leaking. Big problem. What do you do when you run into a problem? Probably tell your close friends, spouse or colleagues. Maybe you seek professional help. If it fails, you try other people's suggestions. If those fail, and you are faced with the prospect of the worst, probably that's when you seek the Lord's help if He can do anything. That's very sad, yet that's what many of us do. That's one of the things Paul was talking about in Galatians 2:21NLT when he said "I do not treat the grace of God as meaningless. For if keeping the law could make us right with God, then there was no need for Christ to die." Unbelief is treating the grace of God as meaningless. Simply put, you have the ability, but you don't want to use it. Other versions use the words nullify or frustrate the grace of God. Unbelief frustrates the grace of God.

Unbelief hinders God from pouring out the benefits of resting in Him. In Jesus' very own town, Matthew 13:58ESV says "And he did not many mighty works there because of their unbelief." Jesus wanted to do more for his hometown, but unbelief hindered him. At times reading this you may say if Jesus was in my town, I would let him heal me and perform as many miracles as he possibly can. Honestly, how could they hinder him through unbelief? You're right my good friend. It's your opportunity. Now Jesus is not only in town, but He now lives in you.

First Corinthians 3:16 NASB says "Do you not know that you are a temple of God and that the Spirit of God dwells in you?" God lives in you; Jesus lives in you and the Holy Spirit lives in you. The problem is you don't believe that. Just like in His hometown, Jesus cannot do many miracles in you because of your unbelief. You are now His hometown. You are His dwelling place. He wants to express His love and grace, all His goodness to you. He wants you to be rested so that He can do it to His overflowing satisfaction. I pray that the Holy Spirit emphasises this truth more and more in your heart. God loves you; you are His righteousness, and He wants to help you in every way.

Hebrews 3:12NIV says "See to it, brothers and sisters, that none of you has a sinful, unbelieving heart that turns away from the living God." Unbelief is classified in the same realm as sin. Unbelief turns away from God. Notice that God doesn't turn away, but an unbelieving heart is the one that does so. Verse 18 and 19 just nails it "18And to whom did God swear that they would **never enter his rest** if not to those who disobeyed? 19So we see that they were not able to enter, **because of their unbelief**."

Unbelief is a hindrance in accessing rest. The children of Israel in the desert failed to enter that place of complete security, supply and health – a place of rest because of their unbelief. Most of them died in the wilderness and never saw the promised land except Joshua and Caleb. Unbelief robs you of your destiny. The land of Canaan was already theirs; God had already given it to them. The land flowing with milk and honey was already theirs, they just needed to believe God, walk the wilderness and get it. But what did they do? They grumbled, complained, turned away from God – walking in unbelief. Jesus elsewhere refers to an unbelieving generation as a twisted, corrupt and perverse generation (Matthew 17:17). James also takes it a notch higher by saying if you are neither cold nor hot, you'll never receive anything from the Lord because you are double-minded. Being lukewarm is having elements of hotness while maintaining those of coldness, you belong to neither.

Sinners, cold as they are, receive from God when they recognise how much they need Him and then His grace flows mightily through them. Just look at how Jesus ministered to sinners and they were healed and saved. Also look at how the fired-up believers of the New Testament in the book of Acts walked in love, miracles and continuous joy. They were hot for Jesus, and they received more. Sadly, some had upheld the law – the Pharisees. They knew every scripture but were somewhere in between, neither cold nor hot, in unbelief. They received nothing from God. Where do you belong to today? Do you trust the Word as it is? Then go for it and start receiving the benefits of resting in His Word.

In the following chapter, I'm explaining why it is possible to have rest and yet not be at rest. This will change your life forever. It changed mine, I believe the same will happen to you. I have called it the two dimensions of rest.

6 | Two Dimensions of Rest

Jesus introduced us to two dimensions of rest. It is truly just one dimension of rest with two dimensions to it, so for our understanding, we have to split it into two kinds of rest. Rest is a person. Jesus Christ himself! In Him was life and that life was the light of man. Jesus Christ the man is the fulness and overflow of rest and He gives it to whosoever desires freely for no charge. If Jesus is resting, how come you still feel restless even though you are born again and believe in grace? Jesus now lives in you; he has his permanent residence in you so why are you restless? These questions are very good, and they are the kind of questions you should always have. This brings us to the two kinds of rest. Let's have a look at this wonderful verse:

> **Matthew 11:28-30NIV** "28"Come to me, **all** you who are weary and burdened, and **I will give you rest.** 29take my yoke upon you **and** learn from me, for I am gentle and humble in heart, and you **will find rest** for **your souls**. 30For my yoke is easy, and my burden is light."

Jesus was preaching to ordinary people in Galilee, who were not necessarily believers but most probably unbelievers. Nevertheless, no one was born again because Jesus had not yet died. He was addressing people that needed a saviour. People that were ravaged by sin, the lust of the flesh, sickness, disease, pain with no solution in sight. People that had been exposed to righteousness of the law and remained in condemnation, in constant guilt and torment. In his message, he reveals two **dimensions of rest**, rest for your spirit and rest for your soul.

Ok, let us go back to the above verse and notice something. Jesus calls all the "weary and burdened" to come and receive rest. Sin had wearied and burdened mankind ever since Adam fell in Genesis. There had never been a solution to the sin problem. The law could not make anyone righteous, rather it brought condemnation. It couldn't defeat sin, instead, it became an environment to make sin very sinful; sin became alive because of the law (Romans 7:9). Jesus is addressing Jews who knew the law and had been burdened and wearied by the many rules and regulations in trying to deal with sin. He is introducing a solution to this big problem. He was the solution. He had a precious gift they did not deserve. A gift that would solve all their problems and bring them to a place of tranquil rest. That gift was himself – Jesus Christ. Jesus said to the unsaved Jews "Come to me…I will give you rest".

Given rest - Rest for your spirit

Salvation is that rest that your spirit needs. It can never be accomplished in any other way apart from receiving Jesus Christ as your own Lord and personal saviour. This rest can only be received. You can't work to get it. It is unmerited, unearned and totally undeserved. Everyone has equal access to it if they believe. The whole world needs this rest and the great commission that Jesus gave in Matthew 28:16-20 is a responsibility for believers to let the whole world aware that this rest is available for free. Isaiah 55:1-2NIV is another glorious verse about this wonderful gift of salvation that brings rest. It says

> "1"Come, all you who are thirsty, come to the waters; and you who have no money, come, buy and eat! Come, buy wine and milk without money and without cost. 2Why spend money on what is not bread, and your labour on what does not satisfy? Listen, listen to me, and eat what is good, and you will delight in the richest of fare."

He is calling (1) the thirsty and (2) those without money. Ok, have you ever been naturally thirsty? How restless do you become? You become excessively restless because you know without another drop of water you are dead meat, right? And secondly, we live in a world whose mode of trade is money. We use money to purchase almost everything from food to accommodation, mobility to and from work for most people. Money is an important factor in our daily lives. Without money, a lot goes undone. Its absence becomes a source of restlessness in so many ways. This call in Isaiah 55 is to the restless who need a saviour. Jesus Christ is that saviour that will give that rest. On that verse he says, I quote "Come, buy wine and milk **without money and without cost**". He is saying you can access as a free gift all those things that give you restlessness. Anything you receive without payment is a gift.

This was written in the Old Testament as a shadow of the reality which is Christ. Only Jesus is the true rest that is received without money and without cost. You get saved, healed, receive the Holy Spirit, speak in new tongues, receive various gifts of the Spirit…and in all this, no money no cost. How wonderful is that? That is received rest. And received rest is domiciled in your spirit. At salvation, your spirit is regenerated to become like Jesus, in all its purity and holiness. That is true rest.

Spirit, soul and body

To fully understand these two dimensions of rest you must understand who man is. What is man's make-up? Are you just a heap of flesh who lives to eat, hustle and die? That's what many realists and atheists think. But nothing is further from the truth. When someone dies, we say he or she's gone, yet we will be looking at their body. At their burial, we lay their body to 'rest' and yet the actual person was totally gone – their feelings, emotions cannot be experienced anymore. Friends, you are not just a heap of flesh. You are more than that. A human being is a spirit being who possesses a soul (i.e. mind, emotions and feelings) and lives in a created body. In the beginning, God created man "out of the dust of the ground". The body originated from the ground, that's why when the spirit departs, we return the body where it belongs – simple hey! King Solomon tries to explain it in Ecclesiastes 12:6-7NIV saying:

> "and the **dust returns** to the ground it came from, **and the spirit returns** to God who gave it."

In Genesis 3:19 it says:

> "By the sweat of your face You will eat bread, till you return to the ground, because from it you were taken; For you are dust, and **to dust you shall return**."

The body is separate from you, when you go it goes back to where it came from, the ground! In Acts 7:59-60BSB, when Stephen was stoned to death the Bible had this to say:

> "While they were stoning him, Stephen appealed, "Lord Jesus, **receive my spirit**. 60Falling on his knees, he cried out in a loud voice, "Lord, do not hold this sin against them." And when he had said this, he fell asleep.""

The phrase 'he fell asleep', in our language today, simple means he died. But pay attention to what he said earlier – he said 'Lord, receive my spirit'. This was exactly what happened to Jesus when He 'gave up His spirit'. Luke 23:46NIV has the account of Jesus' spirit being separated from his body, again, I quote

> "Jesus called out with a loud voice, "Father, into your hands I commit **my spirit**." When he had said this, he breathed his last."

The Psalmist goes on again to clarify the make-up of man in Psalm 146:3-4NIV

> "3Do not put your trust in princes, in human beings, who cannot save. 4When their spirit departs, they **return to the ground**; on that very day, their plans come to nothing".

Wow, this is so simple yet powerful. When the spirit of a human being departs, their bodies return to the ground. So, the scriptures continue to make emphasis of the spirit being separated from the body or rather emphasising that man is predominantly a spirit being living in a body. Stay around while we explain this, it will liberate you. Man was still a heap of flesh until God breathed on him. Genesis 2:7KJV says:

> "And the LORD God formed man **of the dust of the ground** and breathed into his nostrils the breath of life; and man became **a living soul**."

Before God's Spirit (breathe) came into man, man was a heap of flesh with deadness. That verse introduces a new term we have not touched, soul. The Hebrew transliteration of that word, nephesh, defined as soul is broadly defined as "a soul, living being, life, self, person, desire, passion, appetite, emotion" by the NABS exhaustive concordance. Notice that "man became a living soul" only after his body had a spirit. Before that, he was just a heap of flesh. I love Maths, so I would create a simple equation, for understanding, and say spirit plus body equals your soul (Spirit + Body = Soul). So, God created the body with everything it needed, which includes desire, passion, appetite, emotion, etc – you're right, that's your soul. He created your body with your soul in it. But that part of your body is inactive without you, the spirit. Your soul and your body cannot function without a spirit. Man is a spirit, lives in a body made from the ground and possesses a quality called a soul. The spirit aspect of man is that part of him that knows God.

God's spirit brought life to the soul and the body. Now, let's go further and understand things. A human spirit can either be governed by God's spirit or the demonic spirits. When Adam sinned, it was his spirit which was corrupted, which further brought death, sickness, disease, pain, restlessness, stress, etc. to the soul and the body. When he sinned, he literally gave Satan legal right over the government of his spirit. God had told him the day he sinned he would surely die (Genesis 2:17). That was reference to his spirit being separated from God. When man became a new creation according to 2 Corinthians 5:17 or became born again according to John 3, it was his spirit man who became regenerated and reborn.

At salvation, your spirit receives God's life – Jesus Christ – and becomes alive again. This is called being born again, it happens in your spirit part of you. With the above explanation of spirit, soul and body, you now understand what being born again means. Jesus lives in your spirit, in that part of you that knows God. Understanding this will help you reconcile a lot of verses that say we are holy, righteous, like Jesus etc even when our actions may not fully agree with that.

In the same way, now that man's spirit was made righteous, it didn't mean that automatically his soul and body were made righteous. What it meant was that the new condition of his spirit will now affect his soul and body to be in the same likeness. Salvation is that gift of rest for your spirit. You can't earn rest for your spirit, it's impossible! Only Jesus can give it to you. This kind of rest is a gift. A gift into your spirit. Jesus says: "I will GIVE you rest". You don't have to labour or do anything to get this rest. I call it a "given" rest. It is a gift that Jesus gives. It is rest that comes at salvation.

When you believe in the Lord Jesus, as one sent from God to take away your sins, saving you from eternal separation from God, and that God, by the Holy Spirit raised him from the dead, you receive this rest. Your spirit becomes revitalised, alive. It is imbued with life, God's life, His eternal life. 2 Corinthians 5:17 says you become a new creature, or more specifically a creature that never existed before. Given rest makes you a unique creation whose spirit resembles Jesus Christ the last Adam, not the fallen first Adam. Rest for your spirit is a guaranteed GIFT given by Jesus. The demon possessed and oppressed are set free. Their spirits can now operate without the domain of Satan and his schemes. How beautiful is that? This is called REST, finally you can rest from that torment of evil on your emotions, mind, etc. Rest in your spirit is a gift in the same way righteousness is a gift into your spirit (Rom 5:17). Just to remind you, if it is a gift it means that it is free. Hallelujah; Glory to God.

Don't let anyone rob you of this perfect gift of God's rest into your spirit by judging you based on your actions. People judge you based on your failures to discount you from having that gift of eternal life in you, which is the 'given' rest that Jesus talks about. Good or bad actions, I have eternal life in me. Confess that truth until it becomes a reality. You have rest for your soul. You can safely declare that your spirit has eternal security independent of your actions. For as by one man's disobedience (Adam) many were made sinners, so by the obedience of one (Jesus) shall many be made righteous (Romans 5:19).

You see the devil wants you to focus on the weakness of your flesh so that he diverts your attention from whom you truly are now in your spirit. You are a rested, totally peaceful and prosperous person, whose redemption in Jesus Christ is secure forever. That's what Hebrews 9:12NLT affirms saying "With his own blood-- not the blood of goats and calves--he entered the Most Holy Place once for all time and secured our redemption *forever.*" That gift can never be taken away from you. And don't allow anyone to dissuade you and convince you otherwise. Grace has brought you to rest! And it is all for free.

Given rest is totally free, totally supplied by grace! Remember, that rest is domiciled in your spirit. but you are three in one - spirit, soul and body! What about the position of your soul and your body? At what point do these rest? Is your soul and body at rest just because your spirit is at rest? This reminds me of some of the greatest frustrations earlier in my faith in Jesus. I was happy in my spirit, feeling liberated and blossoming in wisdom and knowledge in Jesus Christ, yet most things around me seemed to be contrary. How do you reconcile the two?

Found Rest - Rest for your soul

Jesus continued the same verse in Matthew 11:29-30 to stretch his message of rest. He says, I quote verse

> 29, "Take my yoke upon you **and** learn from me, for I am gentle and humble in heart, and you **will find rest** for **your souls**. 30 For my yoke is easy, and my burden is light."

Ok, let me explain this, you probably understand it, but I will re-emphasise this. Initially, to receive rest you had to be "weary and burdened" and just receive. Remember that? Jesus said come to me all who are weary and burdened and he will give you rest. Given rest, right? Ok, in verse 29 its different. There are two conditions to experience this next dimension of rest, I call it the "found rest". The condition is (1) take my yoke and (2) learn from me. I will stretch these shortly. Once these are fulfilled, He says then "you will find rest for your souls". Wow, really? Yes, beautiful and clear. This is not rest for your spirit, no. It is rest for your soul.

Your soul is the domain of emotions, feelings, your mind and your will. God wants your emotions, your mind and your will to be at rest in Him. You see, this means you can be a restless born again Christian unless you "find" rest for your soul. Rest in your spirit does not guarantee rest in your soul.

There is a part that you play here. And that part has nothing to do with securing or earning that rest, no! The part you play is about finding what has already been made available. Rest is Jesus Christ! Jesus says it is you who finds the rest. The rest for your emotions, mind and will is "found". What does it mean? Where is it hidden? Good question. It is hidden in Jesus. Two things give you access – taking His yoke and learning from Him.

I hear someone saying but pastor, I am a radical grace believer. I am saved by grace through faith and I don't have to do anything but just receive. Ok, I agree with you. That verse you quoted is Ephesians 2:8, it correctly stipulates that salvation is rightly by grace. But how is it accessed? How is it received? Friends, it is received "through faith". Faith is the vehicle to appropriate what grace has provided for free. Grace has provided rest for you, totally free. In Romans chapter ten the Apostle Paul guides us on being saved. He says that "you believe in your heart and confess with your mouth then you will be saved." While salvation is made available free of charge, only those who access it can benefit from it. That accessing is called faith. That's where the key is. You've got to do something to experience rest for your soul folks! That rest is hidden; it needs to be found. Are you ready to find it?

In Romans chapter twelve the Apostle Paul again says "Do not conform to the pattern of this world but be transformed by **the renewing of your mind**. Then **you**

will be able to test and approve what God's will is—his good, pleasing and perfect will." You see the renewing of the mind is where the process of finding rest takes place. Right, you get it, it's a process. It's not instant. While there is only one rest, for your spirit it is received while for your soul you got to find it. It is the same rest but different dimensions of accessing it. This one is NOT a gift; you labour to find IT. Hebrews 4 says let us "labour to enter His rest". This is the only part in the Bible that emphasises labouring under grace, under the New Covenant.

The apostle Paul says when your soul – your mind in this instance – is renewed, you get new abilities. An ability to (1) test and (2) approve God's will – that it is (1) good (2) pleasing and (3) perfect. Why am I bringing this to your attention? Your soul is driven by your will power. God never took away man's will. Man needs to test God's will versus his own will and get to a point of approving that God's will is superior. This can only happen when man's spirit is born of God and when his soul has been renewed by God's word. I will look at this in-depth in the next chapter, again you'll love this.

Before I look at finding rest, let me summarise and put into perspective what we learnt. Jesus gives you rest as a gift into your spirit at salvation. It is free, you don't labour for it. Since you are spirit, soul and body your soul gets to find rest through taking the cross and learning from Jesus. Finally, for the body. Your body was made to respond to the state of your mind. While sleeping is meant to be a form of rest for your body, if your spirit and your mind are restless, your body remains restless too. That's why your body becomes prone to lots of diseases and un-wellness. While body exercise is good, God's word elevates the wellness of spirit and soul as the better more important part. The verse is 1 Timothy 4:8NIV, it says "For physical training is of some value, but godliness has value for all things, holding promise for both the present life and the life to come." You notice it says godliness has value for ALL things. Godliness reflects the condition of your soul and spirit. If those two are great, well and rested in Christ the body becomes responsible, great and equally able to rest effectively. Now let us stretch how you find that rest, which is already a gift into your spirit, for your soul.

7 | Finding Rest for your soul

I remember during the writing of this book I spoke to my wife on the phone and she said to me 'Sbanga, grace works'. She had been so restless about something and finally got to a point of resting in Jesus' ability to open doors. Unexpectedly, Jesus gave her far more than she expected. It was such a pleasant phone call when she said those words. You see grace brings rest to your spirit, but you have a responsibility to transition this rest to your day to day life. I'm talking about rest at work, school, at home in the kitchen, bedroom, living room, everywhere. Religion is bad and ugly. It teaches you fantastic theories that cannot be translated into everyday life. The Good News of God's grace is way lot wonderful. It can be experienced mightily in everyday life.

How then do you find this rest? Jesus gives us the answer. He says, "take my yoke", which means allow me to control you – Let me be truly Lord. You see, a yoke in Bible days was in the **shape of a cross** and the word yoke means **"to be under the authority of"**, or **"to be joined together with"**. For you to be at rest in your soul, you consciously allow yourself to be under the authority of Jesus AND be joined together with him. Your will recognises that the will of Jesus is superior over yours and then you allow the will of Jesus to run every aspect of your life. That will of Jesus is portrayed in a document called the New Testament, His Word. The Word of God, which is the Word of His grace, reveals the will of God to man. Now that is labouring to enter rest, labouring in the Word. Faith, which is belief in the word of His grace, comes by hearing and hearing the words of Christ.

Constant hearing of the words of Christ will eradicate unbelief and establish faith in your heart. Faith is where you have convinced your mind that what the Word of God says is true and will guide your everyday life. Unfortunately, many believers want rest as a gift to their spirit man and to their souls. But it is not so. Rest is freely given to your spirit but needs to be found by your soul. If that were the case, then God would force march everyone to salvation. But God has given you the will power to choose for yourself.

'Found' rest is accepting to live in complete dependence on Jesus: on His protection, supply, provision, health – that is the yoke he's referring to trusting Him. While receiving rest for one's spirit, many believers are so happy; but when it comes to their soul – emotions, mind and will – the responsibility involved, they are very sad. Very, very sad. Jesus wants you to give up your life – your methods, viewpoints, trust, goals, dreams and visions. He wants you to take up His methods, viewpoints, trust, goals, dreams etc. When ploughing, using yoked oxen, the oxen do not just run all over the place. Their movement is controlled. They work when it's time to work and rest when the farmer says so. So, it is with Jesus too. Cease control of your life and give it to Jesus. He gives us a perfect example when He was in the garden of Gethsemane, when soldiers were after His life. He said "Father, if you are willing, take this cup from me, yet not my will, but yours be done." (Luke 22:42NIV).

Jesus had His own will, but He made a conscious choice to let God have his will. That is true resting in the knowledge, wisdom and ability of the Father. I'll give you an example. Jesus wants us to love the way He loves, not the way we think love is. Our love is usually selfish, domiciled around ourselves, our children and/or spouses. But Jesus' love stretches and goes like this: "But I tell you, love your enemies and pray for those who persecute you" (Matthew 5:44). If you are yoked with Jesus, totally under His authority you'll trust His judgment because you have tested His will and found it perfect and good. You'll do this knowing that it is the only way to find rest for your runaway emotions, your soul. That is a practical example many don't want to hear about.

Again, In John 6:38, Jesus gives us another example of what He means. He says, "For I have come down from heaven not to do my will but to do the will of him who sent me." He was completely dependent on the will of the Father. The Father's will had become His own will. He abandoned being led by his feelings and thoughts and submitted those to God. Some people boast of how emotional they are, in a negative way, as if that glorifies Jesus. It makes me wonder how much of their emotions have been handed to Jesus. The starting point of finding rest for your rollercoaster emotions is to give up ownership of your life to Jesus. This is not just accepting Jesus as your own Saviour. It means allowing Him to oversee your soul and your body too. Scriptures like 1 Corinthians 6:19 which says "Do you not know that **your bodies** are temples of the Holy Spirit, who is in you, whom you have received from God? **You are not your own;**" show that a life of found rest goes as deep as touching your body.

You give up ownership of your body. Your spirit is His, totally rested in Him. You renew your mind and train it to submit to the will of God's word, then you surrender your body by choosing that it is not your own anymore. In other words, be under His authority, literally. Be joined together with Jesus. There is no other way, unfortunately, or fortunately. Grace is all about trusting Jesus' ability to run your everyday life. Rest is truly about trusting Jesus' ability. How do you come under the authority of Jesus? It is by His word. When the Word of God becomes the initial, every day and final authority of every aspect of your life, then we are talking.

The church is in a sad state of people with 'received' rest and none of the 'found' rest. So, the outcome of their lives exhibits restlessness, arrogance, and all forms of ungodliness. I'm shocked that some believers swear. Yes, they use all those 'bomb' words. But why? These are believers who serve in the church they even speak in tongues. They are doing everything except being under the authority of Jesus. They still express themselves the way they want, not how Jesus wants. I have pastored people that have shocked me. People that will put you under duress with threats of leaving the church if you insist on Jesus' will on their lives. Satan has deceived them to think that their presence in a body of believers benefits the church leadership more than them. So, they remain controlled by unclean spirits. This is very sad. On the same vein, I will say I have also pastored many wonderful people whose lives are so embedded on Jesus that as a pastor I develop godly envy of a surrendered life. By observing the outcome of their lives, you notice the beauty of the works of grace. How happy and liberated they are!

Whenever there is a gradient of honour, learning is natural. When you go to university, the reputation of that university and the proven quality of the lecturers give you confidence that they will produce a fine competitive professional in you. Subconsciously, you create a gradient to receive teaching from these lecturers because you trust them. In the same way; it takes trusting Jesus and recognising His ability to offer help in running your life. Jesus calls it taking up your cross. When you trust Him, He then says, "learn from me", be my student, be the student of God's word. Be the student of His unearned favour.

Over the years I have pastored believers who will never take a solution from God's word. They will sing in church, pray, attend events etc. but never take a solution from the scriptures. They will want me to pray for them to get breakthroughs, but never to utilise His Word. The bible calls it self-righteousness. Sometimes believers have believed in the man of God more than the God of the man. In other words, God is saying let me be your informer. Do life based on what you hear from me. The life of rest is not a life of striving. It's a life of constant communion with the father. This is the life of a believer! It doesn't demand unrealistic expectations but is at peace with Jesus. It is not led by human manifestations, miracles, etc., but is led by God's Spirit. For example, A restless life prays because there is a problem, gives because there is a need, reads the Bible topically because you need solutions in that area --- That's not rest at all! A restful life is doing all these things because you love the Father, you love Jesus. The issue here is the motive! You pray, study the word, give because it is your lifestyle of fellowship. The motive is love.

Ok, look at it this way. Imagine if your child or your spouse only spoke to you when they wanted something from you. As long as they felt they were ok, they ignore you. They never say good morning, good night, never. But when they run out of gas or petrol and need your help then you see a missed call from them. When they are hungry and they can't fend for themselves, then you get a knock on the door. If it's your spouse, you only hear them call you honey, sweetheart or that pet name when they want something from you. After they get it, they are gone. I've met people like that. Usually, after they have left you to feel awful and abused. That's what many believers do with God. They have a relationship but no fellowship. Full of activity but no rest. The children of Israel were like that and God was not happy with them. Jesus quoted Isaiah in Matthew 15:8 saying "These people honour me with their lips, but their hearts are far from me"

Psalm 20:7 shows a man who understood and had found rest in God. He says, "Some trust in chariots and some in horses, but we trust in the name of the LORD our God." He had given up trust on natural things, just to depend on God, totally resting on his ability to supply and protect. The apostle Paul, during great persecution, wrote to the Corinthians a touching letter, also expressing his total dependence on Jesus. This is what he had to say: "8We think you ought to know, dear brothers and sisters, about the trouble we went through in the province of Asia. We were **crushed and overwhelmed beyond our ability to endure**, and we thought we would never live through it. 9In fact, we expected to die. But as a result, **we stopped relying on ourselves** and **learned** to rely only on God, who raises the dead. 10And he did rescue us from mortal danger, and he will rescue us again. We have placed our confidence in him, and he will continue to rescue us."

This is phenomenal. Even Paul, a master of grace, at some point was depending on his own strength, to the point that he had to 'stop relying on himself and learned to rely on God'. We labour my brethren to find this rest in Christ. We do this by 'learning from Jesus'. Remember He said; 'learn from me', and the apostle Paul says he also had to 'learn to rely on God alone'. This is rest. A life of grace is a life of rest. It's impossible to continue living reckless lives in the name of grace, no ways. Grace teaches us a glorious life of reflecting the character and person of Jesus by constantly depending on Him for all things. And this is effortless when you rest and find the will of Jesus more superior and perfect than yours. It ceases to be a "my pastor said" and starts to be a "Jesus said". Or 'in our church, we don't do this' to 'I don't do this because Jesus tells me so in His Word'. This is rest.

Rest is not governed by rules and regulations; it is governed by love revealed in the scriptures. A life of rest is secure, successful and constantly prospering. John says I wish above all things that you may prosper as your soul prospers. You are secure in relationships, marriage, in your church, everywhere – totally at REST. King David understood this when he wrote Psalm 23. It amazes me because God called him "a man after my own heart" - a heart of REST! Let's have a look at the language of a man who found rest in God. It turns out that those who have found rest have a different language than those who haven't.

8 | A Psalm of Rest

David was a prophetic man. His psalms stepped into the New Covenant, highlighting key tenets of it. Psalm 23 is probably the most popular. David wrote like a new creation believer while he was still in the old testament. Which is why old testament prophets wondered what manner of people living in the New Covenant will be. Let's have a line by live view of the twenty-third Psalm using the NIV below:

> **1 The Lord** is my shepherd, I lack nothing. **2 He makes** me lie down in green pastures, **He leads** me beside quiet waters, **3 He refreshes** my soul. **He guides me** along the right paths for his name's sake. **4** Even though I walk through the darkest valley, I will fear no evil, for **You are with me**; your rod and your staff, they comfort me. **5 You prepare** a table before me in the presence of my enemies. **You anoint** my head with oil; my cup overflows. **6** Surely your goodness and love will follow me all the days of my life, and **I will dwell** in the house of the Lord forever.

In verse 1 of the psalm, David completes his position with God. The Lord IS my shepherd. Wow. This is epic. Rephrasing that, David is saying "The one who owns me is the one who guides me, so I have everything that I need". Dear friend, can you confess like that today, literally? Are you truly owned by God? A life of grace is a life of being owned and dependent on God's ability to live your life for you. The apostle Paul appropriately agrees when he says in Galatians 2:20 "…I no longer live, but Christ lives in me…" that's a bold declaration that he is owned by Jesus. That's the declaration that God is looking for from you. That's the starting point of finding rest for your soul, rest which you already have in your spirit. I discovered that most of the prayer requests are for things God has already given us.

We are trying to get what we already have. You see verse two can never be true in your life if verse one is not true. You can be born again and remain restless because you have not allowed "to be owned and guided" by Jesus. In the western world, where an average person is not poor, you hear people saying they live in lack. Yet you go to some "poor" countries and you see people with almost nothing so happily declaring "they lack nothing". Lack is not about owning properties; it is about "being owned or not". It's not about what you have or don't have, it's about who has you. Jesus came that you and I may have life and have it more abundantly. Let Him own and guide you today. His word is where you get informed and subsequently get guided.

Most of the needs we have border around provision and peace. Look at verse 2. When you have Jesus as your owner and guide you know that you are in constant supply! It is easy for Him to "**... make** you **lie down** in green pastures" and also "**lead** you beside **quiet waters**". This is wonderful. This is glorious. It is beautiful. It is amazing! It is truly lovely. Summarising that verse in other words, we can say Jesus makes us rest in a place of abundance and peace. In this world, when you have abundance and wealth, you have a reason to be restless.

What if I get sued, robbed? We go for the most expensive insurance. At times we don't sleep at night. As long as you don't recognise Jesus as the source of all you have you, have a reason to be restless. What if this or that? But verse two shows us that we don't use our effort to be at rest, He uses His effort. It is Him who "makes me" lie down. I don't make myself. I don't use my effort. I don't try because the more I try the more I fail. I let Him take me to that place of abundance. That place already exists. God wants you to trust Him in taking you to that place. Allow Him to make you rest in His supply and provision. His Word, the word of His unmerited, unearned favour, the word of His goodness will make you "lie down", be at rest. The problem is that we believe this but never action our beliefs. Belief without action is faithlessness.

Acts 20:32 NIV, the apostle Paul addressing elders says, "Now I commit you to the *word of His grace*, which can build you up and give you an inheritance among all those who are sanctified" The *word of his grace* is revealed in the New Covenant. It is that word that will "build" and "give" you what is already there – the inheritance. Do you see that? The green pastures are already there; quiet waters already exist. Only allowing Jesus, through the word of His grace, will make you rest in that place of peace and provision. It is my prayer as you continue reading that you notice and embrace this amazing liberating truth for yourself.

When we continue reading the psalm, it becomes clear that all we try to do ourselves God is willing and ready to do it **only** if we let him do so. Verse three says "**he refreshes** my soul. **He guides me** along the right paths for his name's sake." Are you feeling depressed, disoriented? Anti-depressant pills are not the solution. They can make you sleep and "forget" but truly can't deal with depression. Jesus does. And He wants to. He brings refreshment to your soul; isn't that good. He refreshes my emotions, mind and my will. Ever used a computer, on the internet and a page stops loading? Then you refresh it, what happens? It loads. Your life may be stuck right now. You have clicked every link of going forward, but everything is "un-clickable". Let Jesus refresh your life right now. You can pause reading and take some time to pray in the spirit.

Why am I saying so? Because His word of His grace has a solution for such situations. He says in Jude 1: 20 that we are built up when we pray in the Holy Ghost. Just try it, it works. When believers were tired and weighed down in Acts 4, they prayed, and the result was "they were all filled with the Spirit and preached the Word of God boldly" in verse 31. How pretty is that? Everything we need for this life has already been made available. God wants you to find rest in Him through what He has put in His word. The given rest in your spirit can be translated into your soul only if you let Jesus "own and guide you" literally, by His word.

I would like you to see the last part of this psalm, which is key to continued success and peace in your life. So the Lord, the one who owns you makes, leads, and refreshes you, He guides and is with you, prepares a table for you, all the goodies for this life, and then anoints your head with oil, resulting in your cup overflowing. Hang on, do you notice something? It is the Lord doing all this, not you! That sounds simple hey. In the Old Covenant, it was not that simple. You had to do, to get. For you to qualify to receive all this goodness from God, you had to keep every letter of the law without dropping one. But God's high standard was too high.

Achan in Joshua chapter 7 learnt it the hard way. One sin led to his death by stoning. You see under that covenant, right standing before God was not a gift, it was merited. You had to earn it. Fear reigned in case you did not keep it to the wire. Nevertheless, the purpose of that covenant given to Moses was never to make us righteous but show us that we cannot attain God's high-level standard, so we needed Jesus. Galatians 3:19 puts this clearly and beautifully in the New Living Translation, it says "Why, then, was the Law given? It was given alongside the promise to show people their sins. But the law was designed to last only until the coming of the child who was promised. God gave his law through angels to Moses, who was the mediator between God and the people." So, we no longer have to "do" to be accepted – to reach God's high standard, but we have to "believe and receive" His wonderful grace and gift of righteousness (Rom 5:17).

So, the whole psalm highlights what "the one who owns and guides you" will do for you. I consider it a perfect psalm of rest. I love the last verse, verse six. It says:

> "6 Surely your goodness and love will follow me all the days of my life, and I **will dwell** in the house of the lord forever"

David acknowledges what God will do in his life, and he commits to "dwell" in God's house forever. That was the only commitment He made to God, to dwell. This is all God wants from you and me. To trust Him and His ability to run our lives effectively to the extent that we are so much at rest that we have no other dwelling place apart from with Him. The apostle Peter had a taste of that during the transfiguration before Jesus purchased our salvation. He exclaimed and said "Master, it is good for us to be here. Let us put up three shelters—one for you, one for Moses and one for Elijah" – wow, he experienced in the flesh what is in now in us, God's glory. The beauty of having Jesus living and expressing Himself in us! This will change your life forever! It will redefine why and what you live for. The apostle Paul discovered this reality and "counted" the gains of his life as "dung". Philippians 3:7 would put this clearly, he says "I once thought these things were valuable, but now I consider them worthless because of what Christ has done."

You see when Jesus wasn't in his life, he valued a lot of things of this world. He held them dear in his heart.

But when Jesus came into his life and began to guide and be Lord to him, he realised the immense value of Jesus and what He had done.

Friends, this is too good. If your Christian life is boring, a constant struggle to keep in line, it means something may not be right with your belief system. You may be passionately committed to Christ through the old law that demanded you to do more to get what Christ has made available freely. So, you keep falling short of that required standard. Only through accepting God's grace as a way of life in the New Covenant, learning from Him that reality for you today will you experience true rest.

A life of Rest is a life of dwelling in God, the rest is done by God! A life of rest produces believers who are Christ conscious not self-conscious. When God created heaven and earth, he created man last and placed him in "green pastures" – in a garden that had everything. Man was never created to be stressed. Never! Stress is a by-product of sin and self-effort, trying to do what only God can. After God created man on the sixth day, on the seventh, He declared a holiday of rest. He rested on that day. You see man was created and entered into rest, with God. So, man was never created to be stressed. He was created to be at rest in God's abundant provision in a state of righteousness. This is the very reason why grace came in person (John 1:17), to position us where we belonged, in God's place of abundance and peace, not in warfare with the devil or anyone.

During my early days as a believer, I was around some passionate well-meaning believers who were committed to intense prayer and fasting solely to fight demons, principalities and powers of the dark world. Dethroning Satan and praying at specific times to counter evil traffic. A book called dangerous prayers became dear to me but brought more fear than faith. While I was well-meaning in my passion, I was misdirecting my passion. While Ephesians 6 rightly says our struggle is against all these evil realms, it tells us what our responsibility is in that struggle, that is to stand. Yup, you heard, to stand. Here is verse 13 for you from the NIV, "Therefore put on the full armour of God, so that when the day of evil comes, you may be able **to stand** your ground, and after you have done everything, **to stand**." You see, everything we ever needed, Christ purchased with his blood. He completed everything. Everything! Nothing remained. Romans 8:37 affirms this that we are more than conquerors. Meaning Jesus conquered; so, our job is not to conquer but to proclaim that victory in every sphere of our lives; how sweet! So, our fight is to constantly stand on the victory that Jesus accomplished when He resurrected from the dead. Glory to God!

God provides GRACE so that we can rest in His triumph. Look at it this way. God made all things available for us at Calvary by His blood, now it is up to us to get hold of what is availed for free. I hope I'm talking to someone today. I hope you are prompted to trust the ability of Jesus to bring well-needed rest in your restless life. God wants you to "dwell in the house of the LORD all the days of *your* life, to gaze on the beauty of the LORD and to seek him in his temple" (Psalm 27:4). He wants you in that place of rest, where you can entrust him with all the complications of your life. God loves you, my dear. Surely, he does. It grieves me a lot, I believe even more grief is brought to the Holy Spirit when believers run away from God during difficult times, like unbelievers. Unbelievers don't know where to go during times of crisis, but we do. God has given us an amazing tool called prayer. Because Jesus is alive in us, we can safely and easily talk to him anytime – and that is prayer. Prayer is a wonderful expression that shows we are totally dependent on God's grace. When we pray, we give God leeway to guide us. You see a spirit-filled life is a complete life. It's a life that finds satisfaction in Jesus Christ. It's a life that believes and lives the word. It's a beautiful life. It's a life of rest.

9 | THE SABBATH REST

What makes being a new creation truly the good news is the truth that you enter into God's Rest in comparison to a life of toil and commotion that sin brings. The biggest enemy of mankind was striving against sin. Sin is very bad, and that cannot be over-emphasised. But sin is no longer the problem or biggest enemy for man today. Jesus defeated sin once and for all about 2000 years ago and ushered us into a place of rest by His grace. Romans 6:14 says "For sin shall not have dominion over you: for ye are not under the law but under grace". Grace is Jesus Christ. The New Covenant is based on Jesus Christ, who is the fullness of God's grace to mankind. So because Jesus Christ defeated sin fair and square, once and for all, finally we are free from sin dominion. So if sin is no longer a big problem, then where does the real problem lie?

The biggest problem is refusing to believe that JESUS is the answer or power you need to make you stop the dominion of sin - gossiping, fornicating, witchcraft, poverty, hatred, unforgiveness, etc. – It is called unbelief. Unbelief is like cancer. Nothing good about it. It makes "believers not believe". In Mark chapter 9, a man who had a son who had an evil spirit cried out to Jesus and said: "I do believe; help my unbelief!" There are believers who operate in unbelief – this is an oxymoron. You believe in God, but you don't believe in Him – How is that possible? Look at it this way – You believe the microwave is able to defrost your frozen meat, but you still won't use it. Your actions are in contradiction to what you confess – that is unbelief. You see, when you are in **unbelief**, you are in **unrest**. There is no way you can pray, give, study the word, serve God effectively while living in unbelief – no way! As a pastor, over many years I've seen a trend on many believers. They believe speaking in tongues helps them be edified but they won't speak in tongues when they feel depressed. They believe God answers all things but will miss gathering with other believers when things are hard and will stay away from brethren until "all is sorted out". This is the "unbelieving belief", a weird Christian phenomenon. To truly be set free from unbelief, a believer needs to be at rest in Jesus Christ. I want to show you a full picture from the scriptures on what God intended as rest. We can't talk of REST without talking about the Sabbath!

God Rested

The first mention of Sabbath in the Bible is in Genesis 2:1-2 NIV "1Thus the heavens and the earth were **completed** in all their vast array. 2By the seventh day God had **finished the work** he had been doing; so on the seventh day **He rested** from all his work." Key events preceding **rest** are described by the words **completed** and **finished**. Rest only comes after work has been completed and finished. That's why today's believer can rightly claim to enter God's rest because Jesus cried out and said "it is finished" when He gave up His life for us on the cross.

So God completed and finished all His work of creation within six days and rested on the seventh day, calling it a Sabbath. Now, scholars rightly debate on whether the days of creation were literal 24hr days or were elongated days. I'm not going to get into that conversation in this book, but I want to show you something from the scriptures. The period of creation is chronicled by the words "It was evening, then morning, the 1st day" Have a look at the following verses of creation in **Genesis 1** – Verse 5 (1st day), God called the light "day," and the darkness he called "night." *And there was evening, and there was morning—the first day.*

> Verse 8 (2nd day), God called the vault "sky." *And there was evening, and there was morning—the second day.*
>
> Verse 12-13 (3rd day), The land produced vegetation: plants bearing seed according to their kinds and trees bearing fruit with seed in it according to their kinds. And God saw that it was good. *13And there was evening, and there was morning—the third day.*
>
> Verse 19 (4th day)**,** *And there was evening, and there was morning—the fourth day.*
>
> Verse 23 (5th day), *And there was evening, and there was morning—the fifth day.*

Verse 31 (6th day), God saw all that he had made, and it was very good. *And there was evening, and there was morning—the sixth day*

The seventh day surprisingly is not described in the same way. We are not told of its beginning, neither are we told of its end in a similar fashion the first six days are described. But why? Everything in the Bible has been put for a good reason and our learning. Genesis 2:3NIV says "Then God blessed the seventh day and made it holy because on it he rested from all the work of creating that he had done". I believe this seventh day was Christ concealed. I also believe it was more than just a "day" like the other six. There is no deliberate mention of the start and end of this day. And there is no eighth day mentioned after this "day".

This day is "holy" and "blessed". Abraham met a man "with no beginning of days, no end of life" in **Hebrews 7:3** – His name was called Melchizedek – the Bible calls Him a High Priest forever, resembling the Son of God. Again, this was the pre-incarnate Christ. When Christ had completed securing our salvation on the cross, the Bible says in John19:30NIV "When he had received the drink, Jesus said, "It is finished". With that, he bowed his head and gave up his spirit." The death of Jesus brought the rest that mankind needed so badly, completing the work of a new creation (2 Cor. 5:17) and yet when God completed and finished His work of creation, He rested. The seventh day could be that realm of true rest only found in Christ (Matthew 11:28). It has the tenets of Christ's shadow.

Contrary to popular notion, from creation to Mt Sinai, there is no record that God demanded Saturday to be kept as a Sabbath. While the seventh day represented completeness and finishing, God does not require it to be religiously kept. If it was God's holiday from creation, then all the patriarchs were supposed to honour the day from the onset. As I said, it was more than a day, it was a person, and his name is Jesus Christ.

Only Christ represents the fullness of rest and dominion over sin. Adam, Noah, Abraham, Isaac, Jacob never kept the "day" as a Sabbath day – why? They had a concept of actual rest more than observing a period of time. They never kept the day, but they have a record of honouring and completely trusting in God. Noah rested in the full knowledge that God would bring the flood even though it had never rained on earth. Abraham, fully knowing he was beyond the age of childbearing with his wife, rested in God's ability to give them a son. They understood rest as God himself more than a day.

This is where the importance of separating covenants comes in. The keeping of the Sabbath day commenced in Exodus 16 when the law was given to Moses at Mount Sinai. Commandment number 4 says "Remember to keep the Sabbath day Holy". In Deuteronomy 5:2-3 NIV it says "2The Lord our God made a covenant with us at Horeb. **3 It was not with our ancestors** that the Lord made this covenant, **but with us**, with all of us who are alive here today." He was referring to the Law at Mt Sinai, the law which included the command of keeping a day as Sabbath. This law was supposed to run from Mt Sinai to Christ (Galatians 3:24) and did not cancel or revoke the promise (Galatians 3:17). So Adam, Noah, Abraham, Isaac, Jacob were not under the LAW – That's what Moses was saying – meaning they didn't have to keep the Sabbath for example. You see, God never intended the children of Israel to use the Law as a way of life – It was their arrogance that led God to give them the Law.

Listen to what Hebrews 10:1NLT says "The old system under the law of Moses **was only a shadow,** a dim preview of the good things to come, not the good things themselves. The sacrifices under that system were repeated again and again, year after year, but they were never able to provide perfect cleansing for those who came to worship.

Notice something, everything under Moses was a shadow. Anyone who loves to live Christianity under the law is chasing shadows. Keeping Saturday as a pursuit of Sabbath is in actual truth a chasing "after the shadow" – a dim preview of the good things to come. That shadow is cast by none other than the true rest Himself, Christ Jesus. All the requirements and demands of the law were kept by Jesus Christ our true rest. So when we believe and trust in Him to live out our lives, then through Christ we fulfil the requirements of the law. That's why Paul said, "I no longer live but Christ lives in me".

They will not enter my Rest

While the Children of Israel had been given the seventh day as a Sabbath day, the seventh year as a Sabbath year and that if they keep seven Sabbath years they will enter into Jubilee – the 50th year of debt cancellation. If the faithful keeping of these Sabbaths was meant entering God's rest, then the following verse suggests the contrary.

Psalm 95:10-11NLT "10For forty years I was angry with them, and I said, 'They are a people whose hearts turn away from me. They refuse to do what I tell them.' 11So in my anger I took an oath: 'They will never enter **My place of rest**.'"

Something rings a bell here – while they kept the Sabbaths, they were still not in God's place of Rest! This would then mean there is another rest which is not the Mosaic Rest, it is called **"God's Place of REST"** The writer of Hebrews continues to clarify this

Hebrews 4:8-12 NIV "8 For if Joshua had **given them rest**, God would not have spoken later about another day. **9There remains**, then, a **sabbath-rest for the people of God**; 10 for anyone who enters God's rest also **rests from their works**, just as God did from his. 11 Let us, therefore, **make every effort to enter that rest**, so that no one will perish by following their example of disobedience. 12For the word of God is alive and active. Sharper than any double-edged sword, it penetrates even to dividing soul and spirit, joints and marrow; it judges the thoughts and attitudes of the heart.

So there remains a Sabbath Rest for God's people – now remember who the Book of Hebrews was written to? Yes, you're right, to the "Hebrews" not the Gentiles. So the Jews understood the context of Joshua not giving them true rest. God rested from His work of creation — creating what? Everything that man needed for this life. So when you rest you also rest from *creating everything* you need for this life. What does this mean? It means that instead of depending on your strength to be righteous, healed, promoted, etc. you totally depend on what God has provided freely by His Grace. It means instead of you struggling to overcome sin and its deceitfulness, you totally depend on what our Lord Jesus has already done for us by defeating the power of Sin on the cross — God wants you to reign!

So, what is this Sabbath Rest for God's People?

> Colossians 2:16-17 NLT "16 So don't let anyone condemn you for what you eat or drink, or for not celebrating certain holy days or new moon ceremonies or Sabbaths. 17For these rules are only **shadows** of the reality yet to come. **And Christ himself is that reality**."

Do you see that my friends? Jesus is the Reality of the Sabbath. He is the True Rest that God has for His people. Friends — stop chasing shadows, get Jesus — He is the way, the truth and the life — Your rest! Whenever the children of Israel kept the Sabbath, God supplied *all* their needs, healed all their diseases, provided all their comforts, Its time for that my friends. God wants you to live in homes you never built — rest in Him today! Visas you never deserved, jobs you never qualified for, promotions you never dreamt of — miracles all over! Hallelujah…The whole world needs to hear this marvellous Good News of God's

Rest. Jesus is coming back again. Your relatives don't have to go to hell! Jesus loves them. I said Jesus loves them. God is looking for men who will tell this to the world – that the True rest has arrived. Jesus Christ the Son of the living God has arrived – Hope is here. Rest is not a day; rest is Jesus Christ. You get Jesus, you Are rested from all your labours, hallelujah!

Jesus healed and did good on the Sabbath day because He was the owner, the Lord, of the Sabbath.

10 | Restful Prayer

Some believers who have embraced God's grace with passion have aborted some key elements of walking with our Father such as prayer, soul-winning and giving or generosity. In this chapter, I want to look at prayer. Previously I briefly mentioned my experiences with a book called dangerous prayers. Contents of that book are being expressed in various ministries that have been built on deliverance and special prayers given by special people that have a special effect on its subjects. Mainly the book promises to accomplish what Jesus already did. I had to wake up at night, midnight, and pray facing the east addressing various spirits and demons of witchcraft.

I had to be up again at 3 am to deal with water spirits and the like, witches on their way back from their acts of evil. You see, just the thought of evil and what may happen if I didn't pray motivated me to pray harder in faith mixed with fear, fear in case the devil overcomes me. I lived in the bondage of prayer instead of the liberty of prayer. Here the bondage of prayer means praying out of fear of consequences. There are many people still stuck here. Jesus purchased a better way of life for us. A way of grace. The New Covenant, where prayer is done at rest, knowing that

Jesus has accomplished and dealt with Satan himself and all his host when He "he made a public spectacle of them, triumphing over them by the cross" (Col. 2:15)

This knowledge lets you pray differently. Prayer is key in the life of a believer. Jesus shows us the best example in restful prayer. Responding to Martha, who was worried about Lazarus who had been dead four days, Jesus says "Father, thank you for hearing me. You always hear me, but I said it out loud for the sake of all these people standing here, so that they will believe you sent me." After this, he commanded Lazarus out of the grave and he came out alive. But here is the point; he was convinced that when he prayed the Father heard him. He was so much at rest whenever he prayed.

Now, this is a contrast with many who pray and fast many days hoping to get God to hear their prayers. Jesus was aware, conscious and convinced that all the prayers he made were heard. The power that exuded from that prayer was a result of constant regular fellowship with the father in personal devotion. So He knew the Father always heard Him. It was not trial and error. That's what Jesus purchased for you at Calvary. That every prayer you make He hears. So if that is true, then it is key that you pray with rest, knowing that your loving father hears you. The prophets of Baal cut themselves all day long, crying out hoping to be heard by their god (1 Kings 18). Elijah provoked them and they danced all day long, prophesying cutting themselves till lots of blood flowed.

Sadly, today many believers do the same. For them, prayer is not a time of intimacy with the Father, it's a time of war. A time of battling with things that were defeated more than two thousand years ago. It's a time of convincing the Father to do what He has already agreed to do and has done through Jesus Christ. That's very wrong. It's oppressive. God wants us to be at rest in Him based on what our Lord Jesus has already done. When we pray, we are convinced that He hears us and an answer to the affirmative is guaranteed. That's restful praying there.

The Father's love in restful Prayer

The origin of most oppressive doctrines are misquotations from scripture. And one of the key misquotations of the story of the wicked judge has plunged ministries into endless prayers of intercessions to a God who takes very long to hear us. Again, that is wrong. Let me put this clear. The fact that it feels good to pray in a certain way does not make it right. The Father ordained a beautiful, restful way of praying that liberates the believer. Walk with me as we go through this verse below

> Luke 18:1-7 NLT - One day Jesus told his disciples a story to show that **they should always pray and never give up**. 2"There was a judge in a certain city," he said, "who neither feared God nor cared about people. 3A widow of that city came to him repeatedly, saying, 'Give me justice in this dispute with my enemy.' 4The judge ignored her for a while, but finally, he said to himself, 'I don't fear God or care about people, 5but this woman is

driving me crazy. I'm going to see that she gets justice because she is wearing me out with her constant requests!'"

6 Then the Lord said, "Learn a lesson from this unjust judge. 7Even he rendered a just decision in the end. So don't you think **God will surely give justice** to his chosen people who cry out to him day and night? Will he keep putting them off? **8 I tell you; he will grant justice to them quickly**! But when the Son of Man returns, how many will he find on the earth who have faith?"

Prayer is fellowship with the Father. Jesus was teaching His disciples that they should always have fellowship with the Father. You see fellowship involves talking, listening, doing things together, spending time literally. That is prayer in its simplistic form. It involves asking too. So Jesus, establishing a New Covenant, a new way of life, tells his disciples to never give up on spending time with the Father. He was teaching them this because it was his lifestyle. Prayer was his lifestyle. To emphasise the power of prayer, Jesus gives the above parable using extreme situations to show the power of asking. He uses an example of "an unjust judge, who never fears God nor cared about people" answering a request from a widow. After persistence, this unjust judge responds to the demands of the judge. So the general lesson is if you keep persisting in prayer, it will definitely be answered, right? I agree.

But, hang on there a bit. This story has been misinterpreted by a lot of people to mean that "We should pray HARD until God is convinced we need what we are praying for THEN He will give us" You see, this assumption is based on the fact that our heavenly Father is like this "an unjust judge, who never fears God nor cared about people". But what's the truth about our God? Psalm 34:15NIV says "The eyes of the LORD are on the righteous, and his ears are attentive to their cry". You see the unjust judge's ear was not attentive to the cry of the widow. But our loving heavenly Father is always ready to hear your prayer. In fact, every prayer that you have ever made, God has heard it AND answered it.

The psalmist also says, "Because he bends down to listen, I will pray as long as I have breath!" how sweet is that. But now in the New Covenant, He doesn't bend down to listen as if He is far away as it was before, now He lives in you. He knows your going in and going out. In Matthew 6:8 Jesus told His disciples that "your Father knows what you need before you ask him". You see, He is not far away, separated from you such that you need a special person to intervene and bring you closer to Him and negotiate that you be heard. A big No. It was like that in the Old Covenant, but Jesus turned things around at the cross.

When you are praying now, you are not approaching an angry God of the old covenant who was speaking with "a **voice so terrible** that 'those listening' begged God to stop speaking". No, Jesus changed all that. Hebrews 12:22NIV "No, you have come to Mount Zion, to the city of the living God, the heavenly Jerusalem, and countless thousands of angels in **a joyful gathering**." Wow! So you come to a place of joyful gathering. Your thoughts about God's attitude towards you determines how you pray. If you think He's after condemning you, and going hard after you, then you have every reason to be afraid. But if you know He is a loving Father who sees you through what Jesus has eternally done, then you approach Him with joy and peace knowing that all evil you have done is already forgiven and God is willing to help you overcome all temptation. That is restful praying. That is prayer after the cross. How wonderful. So restful praying doesn't mean no prayer. It means praying with knowledge of the loving gracious nature of God in the covenant of grace.

In concluding the story of the widow and the unrighteous judge, Jesus says our righteous Father "will grant justice to them quickly" unlike the unrighteous judge. This is wonderful. Does this mean when I need something, my Abba Father quickly answers? Absolutely yes! But where then is the problem, I don't seem to see the answer? Probably you're asking. The answer is simple. If you believe wrongly your expectations are wrong so is your life. If you believe God only answers prayer after a long forty-day prayer and fasting, no matter the answer arrives after a day you won't see it because your system does not recognise it.

Your concept of how God operates will determine how to receive. I believe in 7, 21 and 40-day prayer and fasting. I believe it's a beautiful way of fellowshipping with the Father and its highly recommendable. But I don't believe it's a way to arm-twist God to "answer" your "prayers", no. why? Because God has already promised to answer our prayers because of Jesus' sacrifice on the cross. If the Father hears Jesus always, then He hears you always because "Christ lives in you" and you "live in Christ".

Sometime in 1997, I was a radical believer at a boarding school called Northlea High School in Zimbabwe, Africa. I had a very intimate personal fellowship with the Father. During my two years at the school I was nominated to pastor all the students and teach them the Word every week, how sweet. I also founded and established a students' fellowship group for non-boarding students. One day, when I was doing my A-Level, equivalent to Year 12 in Australia, there was what was called a dinner dance.

This was a no holds barred party to the early hours of the morning. Naturally, I was hotly opposed to this and I made my position clear to the school authorities. When the day of the dinner dance came, I attended the dinner. After all the speeches I was publicly escorted out of the "dance" venue so that I "don't interfere". You see my feeling was that it was wrong to usher young people to a world of heavy music and unholy interactions with the opposite sex, so I had told them that I will pray for the dance not to proceed. I remember the day vividly like yesterday. After I was locked up in my second-floor room, I sat down and prayed. I said "Lord, glorify your name and cause the dance to stop because…" before I finished that very short prayer, there was quiet. I stopped praying, looked through the window, and it was quiet. Ten minutes later so prefects came to my room and told me the PA

System had blown and everyone in there believed my prayers had worked! Wow, so God had answered that prayer faster than I expected! Friends, God did it with Jesus, with me and He can do it with you too. He hears every prayer you make, and He answers. You better believe it.

You see, when we talk to the father, we demonstrate to Him how dependent we are to Him, that's why He gave us the gift of praying in tongues too. When situations face us, we declare our authority to those situations because we live a life of constant fellowship. We are assured of a certain victory. So should a believer living under grace pray? This cannot be over-emphasised. In trueness, a believer of the New Covenant should pray without ceasing. Because we are so dependent on the Father on everything. If we don't pray then we are claiming dependence on ourselves, which is self-effort. Living in grace means without Jesus we're nothing.

A prayer-less believer claiming to live under grace is deceiving themselves. A prayer-less life is unsustainable. The apostle Paul admonishes Timothy in chapter two of his first letter, verse two saying "In every place of worship, I want men to pray with holy hands lifted up to God, free from anger and controversy." The apostle Paul, a champion of grace advocated for prayer. God wants it for you too. New Covenant life without prayer is like a brand-new car without fuel. You don't go anywhere.

Restful prayer is the most effective prayer you can give to the Father, and it is full of thanksgiving, worship, love, intimacy, revelation of the WORD, basking in his presence, healing, joyful increase, expansion, Grace everywhere! Restful Prayer is premised on the fact that God will not withhold anything good from those He loves. You say words like "Lord, I thank you that I'm at peace because I have you, I'm healed because you say so, I'm blessed because you live in me, I'm healthy, I'm prosperous, I'm righteous, I'm a king, I'm beautiful, favoured, spreading, successful…Lord, I'm at rest! I'm at rest, constantly supplied. I forgive, I give, I love because your grace is enough for me…"

So, if restful prayer is such a beautiful experience, how many times and how long should a new creation believer pray in a day? You may say Daniel prayed three times a day; so, should we pray three times a day too? Should it be three hours like Jesus in the garden of Gethsemane? This might sound funny, but doctrines and bondages have been established around these and other bible-based examples. Before I give you the Bible opinion of how many times and how long we should pray, I'll ask you a question. Suppose you are married to someone you really love, or you have a parent or child you love deeply. How many times should you talk to them in a day and for how long? Three times a day? What if you see them, bump on them in the kitchen, etc. would you ignore them? Ok, how long should each session be? One hour? You see, the law is restrictive. You wouldn't do that. If you wouldn't, then what makes us think that God would be different. Prayer is spending time with the Father. Restful praying is spending that beautiful time without fear the Father would turn against you. Under grace, there is a time frame to prayer. It is found in 1 Thessalonians 5:16-18 "Rejoice always, pray without ceasing, give thanks in all circumstances; for this is the will of God in Christ Jesus for you."

There you have it! The time frame for prayer is "don't stop praying", put differently is you're constantly living a life of communion with the Father. You are always in prayer. How liberating is that? I love what that verse says also: REJOICE always…PRAY always…GIVE THANKS in all circumstances. Wow, can you see that? Prayer, rejoicing and giving thanks is a lifestyle, not an event. When the Lord revealed this to me it changed my life radically. I couldn't live in condemnation anymore because my alarm didn't ring at 3 am for my warfare prayer. No ways! Actually, I began to worship, pray and commune with the Father in my sleep. This has become so common in my life that almost daily; I wake up worshipping Jesus as a continuation of what was happening in my sleep. That is restful prayer. My friend, I invite you to this glorious life of liberty and joy. A life of rejoicing always, praying always and giving thanks always. You know why? Because it "is the will of God in Christ Jesus for you"

Before I conclude this section you're probably asking, "Pastor Sbanga, shouldn't we follow the example of Daniel, Elijah and other great men of God who prayed, and things happened?". Your answer is simple. All those people were in the old covenant, an old system which was superseded by Jesus. Now the Father lives in us by the Holy Spirit, so we pray like Jesus. One day our Lord Jesus prayed and said in John 11:42 "I knew that You always hear Me, but I say this for the benefit of the people standing here…" Jesus was so much at rest in praying to the Father that He knew always that the Father heard Him. That is the attitude of a believer who lives in restful prayer; they know that the Father always hears them.

So, what does this mean pastor? Should we abandon prayer meetings? No! not at all, no! Prayer in any form benefits us, not God. Remember that the devil cannot encourage you to pray in any form. You see, in the same way you meet to fellowship with your loved one alone for breakfast or lunch, as well as in a group for example as a family, so it is with meeting up with God. At times, you intimately go away and be with God quietly where no one listens, like Jesus will retreat for elongated times of prayer. Or meet Him as a group, like Jesus took Peter, James and John when He retreated to the garden of Gethsemane to pray. Whichever way you meet Him, always make sure you are constantly hearing from Him. That is the life Jesus has given you for free. Group prayer meetings are exciting and beneficial in that when someone is edified, that edification easily ministers to others resulting in the whole group being edified and uplifted in faith. Pray privately, pray as a group but above all let every minute of your life be a prayer!

We see powerful examples of believers praying together and God working miracles within. A beautiful example is when Peter was in prison, and the church gathered in prayer. That humility of seeing God as the source of our solutions releases amazing grace. James 4:6ESV says, "… God opposes the proud but gives grace to the humble." It takes humility to pray, whether as a group or as an individual. When God sees that humility, He gives more grace, Hallelujah! Do you want more grace? Walk in humility. Walk in prayer! Glory to God.

11 | Effortless Testimonies

I'm sitting with my wife discussing a few things on a Wednesday evening when a message comes through my mobile phone, the time was 9:03 pm. Opening the message was three emoticons of someone laughing with joy. The message continued, and I quote as it is: 'I just found the keys this very minute. I wasn't even looking for them and there they were just in front of my eyes. God is good.' This was a lady from our church. She couldn't make it to church the previous Sunday because her daughter had misplaced the car keys on the Saturday night. She had looked everywhere, cleaned the house and done everything to satisfy herself that the keys are not in the house.

With three school going kids and one infant, it was a difficult period for her especially noting the husband had travelled overseas on a business trip. She resorted to borrowing a car seat from a neighbour and using their second car because everything was locked in the other car. On Tuesday, the third day after the loss of the keys, I had asked her how she was going, managing without the car. He response was astounding, I quote: 'Pastor, I have decided not to lose my peace over the matter and trust God that I will find the keys'. That response touched me. I further responded and said, 'That's a beautiful position of rest...well done. The Holy Spirit will guide you to where the keys are'. Her response was 'amen' which means let it be so.

On a Wednesday evening, around 9 pm she later told us that she walked towards the bookshelf looking for a pencil, and what does she find? The keys stacked up there with the books. Wow! She said, 'pastor it was so effortless'. Exactly, that's what the position of rest does. It brings you to that place of peace and trust that God will take care of everything, and in her case, He did. How powerful is that. I love this testimony because it portrays an everyday mum doing what everyday mums do, and in the process, she practises what she is being constantly taught and it works. Friends, God's Word works! God's grace means you are a beneficiary of what you do not deserve. And for you to effectively tap into those benefits, you need to be totally at peace that God 'will do what He said He will do'. That is called rest. Jesus wants you to try Him in this and see that He is good. Psalm 34:8NLT says 'Taste and see that the LORD is good. Oh, the joys of those who take refuge in him!' Simply put God is saying try me out and see if you won't experience my goodness.

Christianity is a life of true rest. It saddens me to see believers who don't believe Jesus can run their lives effectively with success. I see them always, striving hard, coming to church yet totally not liberated to Him. They carry burdens, lots of them. They still feel like they are not delivered from their sins and other oppressions. They go from prophet to prophet, church to church searching for what they already have in them. Due to frustration, some of them see the Word of God with suspicion, as an enemy that wants to rob them of their pleasures. Bogus false prophets haven't made it better for them. The Word of God works friends! Literally, in our day to day lives! Just like it did for this mother of four, the Word can work wonders for you. Try it out today. I have chosen to experience this life for myself, my children and my wife. The Word of God's unmerited favour has radically transformed our lives.

Many believers are afraid to testify when the Lord does something good in their lives. I guess that probably they won't be sure if truly it was God who did it or someone else, or it was them, their own effort. In most cases, they are embarrassed to glorify God in public because they know they participated heavily in acquiring that blessing. I have seen miracles all my life, and I don't stop glorifying Jesus for them. God has used amazing people to fulfil his will in my life. I desire that you experience even more than I have.

We do not testify by chance or collision; we testify by design-effortlessly! Unbelievers and those still stuck in legalism and religion are the ones who testify by accident. To them, life is a game of chance it's all about probability. They faithlessly hope that things will work out! You do what you got to do and wait to hope that you strike a jackpot, they say. And that is the language of the lottery. Have you ever seen people that bet? Some have done it all their life and have won nothing but continue to do it. Now that's called religion. Some of those that have won the lottery have lost most of their money on worthless things, some becoming bankrupt. That's a very sad life. We are not like that; we don't just hope, we know for real things will work perfectly because Jesus says so! There is a key to testifying, it is called rest, and that rest is found in Jesus. When you rest in the provision of Jesus, you liberate Him to work mightily in and through you. The apostle Paul puts it beautifully in Romans 5:17NIV. "For if, by the trespass of the one man, death reigned through that one man, how much more will those who receive God's abundant provision of grace and the gift of righteousness reign in life through the one man, Jesus Christ!" The key word in this verse, in the context of rest, is the word "receive".

We **receive** to reign – not in heaven, but in **this life**. Since the abundant provision of Grace and the gift of Righteousness was acquired for us for free by our Lord Jesus, it means that if we can **receive it**, then we can reign in this life, right? Receiving is an act of **rest**, or a state of **rest**. There is an abundance of grace and the free gift of righteousness that Jesus has given to everyone who believes. It is available, you just need to receive it.

You see, receiving is hard if you are not at rest. How do you testify if you have not received? And how do you receive if you are not rested? The bankruptcy of testimonies in your life is not because God has ceased to bless His people, no! It is because you are not at rest in Him. Restlessness means you can't wait for God's time. Resting does not mean not working. Neither does it mean relaxing. Resting is working with no worries while you work. Resting is working from a position of having received, not of trying to receive – this is key. I'll give an example. My children wake up every morning to clean the house and tidy their rooms; not to get accommodation and food, no. They do it knowing that all is already provided. Their accommodation and meals have been secured whether they clean or not. They tidy their rooms and help with the chores because they love me and their mum, and they're submitted to our authority. They work inspired by our love and the guarantee that all they need is already theirs. That's exactly what our relationship with God has to be. Everything we ever needed; Jesus paid the full price. We serve Him out of rest and love, knowing that all that we need has already been fully secured. When we do that, it glorifies our Father and He avails even more for our enjoyment resulting in many testimonies. It's a different story with a hired servant – they know their food is dependent on whether they work or not.

The woman with the issue of blood, as popularly known should be referred to as the woman who rested in Jesus ability to heal her. The testimony of her healing was restful testifying. She had spent more than twelve years and physicians had failed; she had lost all hope. Touching Jesus, and the healing coming instantly, her life was transformed. She could testify Jesus did it. That is restful testifying. You can't pinpoint exactly how this could have been, apart from God. In our church, we have seen extraordinary miracles of healing and provision as more and more believers embrace this glorious truth of resting and fully relying on Jesus.

Bridget is a young mother living in Australia. Sometime in April 2017 she picks up the phone and calls me. She says, "Pastor, I thought I couldn't text you but call you and fully express my joy", I was like ok, go on. She said, "I went to the bank yesterday and the lady by the counter, after looking at my driver's licence says to me 'do you realise your driver's licence is expiring tomorrow?'" I was like, ok go on. She continued "Pastor, what it meant was that I had to convert my license from Queensland to Western Australia, and in WA you have to undergo an eye test before you are issued with a license".

Friends, up to this point I wasn't getting exactly where she was going. Ok, then she proceeded "so, I went to the department of transport and they made me go through the eye test. Pastor, I did not only pass the test, but the person who was conducting the test also said to me you have very normal eyesight". At this point, her voice was booming on the phone with joy and excitement, and I'm still like 'ok, that's fine, nice, so you got your licence'. I had missed the crux of the story until she said, "Pastor, my healing has been finally fully confirmed. I was nervous because, after the miraculous healing of my eyes, I had not gone to the doctor for a check-up". Glory to God! It was at this point that everything came together, and I saw the basis her testimony.

About two years back I was ministering, and I had called people to come for healing, any condition! I still remember the day. There were almost twenty people with various conditions, some that scared me when I heard them. Bridget was part of that crew. She was wearing these thick prescription glasses and wouldn't do without them. She is a schoolteacher. So, I approached her and declared in the name of Jesus that she was healed. This was after a teaching on how to walk in the freedom of God's health secured by God's grace. Instantly, I told her to remove her glasses. At the time she screamed, "pastor I can see, I can read that, and that, and that!" Wow! And from that day, she never wore those glasses again. You may say, pastor, it's because you are a pastor, you always do this. The answer is no. It was my first time as a pastor to pray for someone with such a condition and they recover instantly.

By the way, there were other people with similar conditions on that prayer line that went home not healed. What made her different is that she allowed the word to work, and it did! So, her testimony was the medical affirmation of what Jesus had done two years earlier. This is glorious. In her testimony, we see Jesus all over it. We see grace written all over. She wouldn't claim she did it, or some doctor somewhere did. She rested in the ability of Jesus to heal her. Friends, the Word works! Walk in rest and let the Word work. You may probably ask in disappointment, why can't God just heal everyone instantly and we all live in health. I will partly answer that with a question and say why the whole world doesn't get saved since salvation is for free. You see, the world chooses not to believe, that's why they do not get that free gift of salvation. It is the same with healing, provision and other areas in our lives.

Percy is a mother of two and lives in Ipswich, Queensland. She is a qualified nurse who sadly couldn't practice in Australia. She went on to study pharmacy and after two years of graduation, she still couldn't get a job. One Saturday morning, she came for a leaders meeting, and boy, did we worship Jesus. On that day, we couldn't discuss even one thing, the glory of the Lord filled our meeting place. We cried, laughed, worshipped and fell in love with Jesus over and over. Amid that, the grace to prophesy was there, and we stepped into it. For sister Percy, the word was very direct. "you are getting a job in line with your profession. Go and apply immediately!" This was insane. I hadn't spoken to her on that. Three weeks on, I get a phone call. "Pastor, I got it". It was sister Percy. Her joy was unspeakable. She went on and on and on, glorifying Jesus.

This is her story. She had been applying for so many jobs and still getting nothing and had almost given up until that meeting. From that day, she trusted Jesus to be her full supply. She made a conscious choice to rest in Jesus' ability to do so and be at peace. Walking from that meeting, she told herself it is done. This job wasn't just a job. It wasn't an entry graduate job, no! The role she got is one that takes eight to ten years on the job for one to be promoted to that role. You see, Jesus restored all the lost years in one go. That is grace! That is a result of resting and letting Jesus be in charge. Her testimony continues.

This job was an hour's drive from her house and was a casual role. We glorified God and said we trust God that she will be made permanent and transferred close to her home. Two months later, I get another phone call. "Pastor, they have just offered me a permanent role!" I was like what? That's too fast, we're still celebrating your first testimony. Amazingly, usually, it would take a long time to be given a permanent role. But Jesus did it. The testimony doesn't stop here. About a month later she called, "I have been offered a transfer to a branch that is 10 minutes from home. Pastor this is glorious". I was in awe. Dumbfounded! And she says, "you won't believe this. They have also offered me a scholarship to do a graduate diploma, worth about $24,000". At that point I realised something, Jesus is at work! My brother, my sister it pays to walk in the rest that Jesus gives.

From a place of no work and no prospects of employment in a very competitive and flooded field, God did not only offer her a good job but a scholarship where she pays nothing back. Resting in Jesus allows Him to work unhindered into accomplishing those things we need so badly. There is grace for you to testify when you rest in Jesus!

I trust that these testimonies show you Jesus. We can't claim any credit. We've grown to be complete in Him. Content in all things. He is our hope, our peace, our joy. I can write a full book of healing and provision testimonies when believers take time to rest in the Lord and in His ability to heal and provide. I will share a few more. In October 2016, I declared it was a month of testimonies in our church. A young lady had been away from her husband for three years and was hoping to secure him a visa to come and join her in Australia. After the first denial, his visa was eventually granted. A big testimony on its own. I'll leave it for another day.

He arrives in Australia and we share with Him what the Lord has been doing in our lives and how yielding totally to the grace of God has produced results. He came to the prayer line. He was two or three days in Australia at the time. The grace to prophesy was there. I told him to apply asap, the Lord has given him a job. This was on a Sunday. On Monday, he was called for an interview, on Tuesday he got a job and on Wednesday he started work. Really? Yes! And it's not done yet. This was a job, but not within his field of expertise. By Friday, he had been called by two top hotels in Brisbane for an Assistant Hotel Manager job. The following week he attended interviews and mid that week he resigned from his job because he had accepted a job as Assistant Night Manager. Within fourteen days! In Australia? With no connections at all. It was Jesus. The best description is that he did not deserve it, and you're right! That's why it is called grace.

Fast-forward six months or so later. This same brother is working hard to provide for his family, totally at rest because of what Jesus has already done for him. His daughter had just arrived to join him and his wife, so he took a week off from work to allow his daughter to settle down in a new country. During those days off something happened at work that results in the position of Night Manager becoming vacant. To cut the long story short, on his first day back from his break he found an offer on his desk, a promotion to be the night manager for the hotel. Not only that, but they also added a further 25% to the salary of what the night manager would usually get. Wow! This is too good to be true, but it is very true.

The brother was gobsmacked! He did not expect it. As I write this, he is constantly glorifying God and has immersed himself as a volunteer in church, an expression of thanksgiving to the Lord. Fast forward to 2020 during the Covid-19 pandemic. While everyone was laid off at his workplace, miraculously he was not laid off. You may say this is a coincidence, but the truth is 'the blessing of the Lord makes rich and does not bring any sorrow with it'.

Another young lady, again in our church, had just walked out of an interview and was feeling depressed because she didn't feel she had done so well. She was a young believer who was growing in the knowledge of God's grace and walking in His rest. She had worked in a nursing home but now wanted to work in a hospital as a registered nurse. Those in the nursing field would understand how challenging that could be. She called me and we had a chat about her interview.

We agreed that 'our success is not based on how well we perform but on how well Jesus performs'. And we agreed that Jesus always out-performs expectations. Instead of worrying she may not get the job, she decided to walk in rest. This was her position, 'If the job is mine, it is mine and no one can take it away. If I don't get the job it means God has something better for me'. So regardless of how the outcome would be, she was firmly positioned in a place of rest, how beautiful is that? A week later, I got the unexpected phone call, 'pastor, I got the job'. What a testimony. So effortless!

All these testimonies are meant to glorify God, and encourage you that God is still at work in the godless societies we live in. I will share a few of my family's significant healing testimonies. My son was born with one kidney and the doctors told us he should never play contact sport. To make it worse they told us that all the associated organs, tissues or cells that make it possible for that second kidney to be there were absent. Fast forward a couple of years later, my wife decided to get into a personal 40-day prayer and fasting. Just before she finished, my son started getting some excruciating abdominal pains. I was away overseas, so I told my wife to take him to the hospital to be looked at. At the hospital they asked for his medical history and eventually decided to check how his kidney was functioning. To their amazement, they saw two kidneys. It was a shock to them and my wife, but not Jesus! When I got back from overseas, we made another appointment to see a renal consultant. They did scans and tests and confirmed that all the associated organs, veins etc had grown and the new kidney was not only functioning well but was almost the same size as the original one. Today my son is a teenager, plays basketball and is as strong as you can imagine. This was effortless!

My wife struggle with fibroids and each year was told that the fibroids were growing. Sometime in 2019 she was told that there was a fourth one and the only remedy was to remove her uterus. Mid 2020 they discovered a cyst in her womb which made an already bad situation worse. In the process we kept confessing the word and Thembi kept listening to a lot of pastor Creflo Dollar's teachings on healing, applying those grace principles in her life. Towards the end of 2020 she was booked for surgery, but her consultant suggested to make a final check of these fibroids using a camera. The outcome of that procedure was probably the biggest shock of our lives, but not with Jesus! The medical consultant said they did not locate any evidence that there was any fibroid in my wife's womb and the cyst had also disappeared, and my wife was no longer in pain. What a medical miracle! She is now painless, and still has her womb intact. Totally effortless, hallelujah! Friends, effortless testifying is real.

Lastly, is my testimony. In 2018 I was diagnosed with a stubborn bug called helicobacter pylori. My general practitioner guided me in taking the first line of treatment, which to my relief effectively reduced the load of the bacteria but did not eradicate it. When I did the tests in 2019, together with some blood tests they found that bacteria loading had significantly increased, and I had issues with my liver which had potential to be cancerous. So I was referred to a medical consultant whom I saw in December of 2020. He conducted an endoscopy procedure to take a biopsy in my tummy so that they could culture and find out what antibiotics would work effectively to eradicate the bacteria. He also instructed me to do additional blood tests and scans to my life.

On the 18th of January 2021 I walked into his rooms at Sunnybank to hear what the treatment plan was going to be. As you guessed it, to the amazement of the consultant and us, he looked at us and said, 'the helicobacter pylori is gone!' It is no longer in your body;

your body has fixed itself!' Our eyes popped out, and he said 'also, your liver has fixed itself, it's in perfect condition! Your body has fixed itself'. At that point my wife couldn't hold her excitement, she responded and said, 'we prayed, it's the power of prayer!'. Once again, this was totally effortless, the works of grace, depending on the finished work!

Friends, we see Jesus at work daily in our lives. You notice that the praise reports in this book involve normal believers living normal lives facing normal problems that normal people face daily and yet they experience God's supernatural hand in those normal situations. And these testimonies span from healing to provision. God wants you to testify! A life of rest is a life of testifying. Such is what we have never seen in our life. A life of rest is a life of grace. A life of being led by the Spirit. A life of depending and loving Jesus. It's a life of ongoing testimonies. If you don't see ongoing testimonies in your life, review the way you believe and what you believe. Probably you are a committed and devoted religious Christian who has done the same things over and over without results. Jesus wants to help you, and it's all for free. You don't have to be an apostle to experience the benefits of a new creation. You need to be you and trust that the Word works, and start applying it in your circumstance.

Some, due to unbelief, may want to dismiss these testimonies as just medical coincidences. Mhhh, then if believing in Jesus positions me into such medical coincidences, then I would encourage anyone to believe in Him.

In the next chapter, you will see how new testament believers overcome their battles. It's totally different from what the church has traditionally taught as spiritual warfare. You want this kind of ammunition in dealing with day-to-day life's problem.

12 | RESTFUL WARFARE

Before we look at this breath-taking story of the fall of Jericho, have a look at this verse.

Psalm 37:7NLT "*be still* in the presence of the LORD and *wait patiently for him to act*. Don't worry about evil people who prosper or fret about their wicked schemes."

I love the King James version...it says, "*rest* in the LORD, and *wait patiently for him*: fret not thyself because of him who prospereth *in his way*, because of the man who bringeth wicked devices to pass."

The psalmist says, 'be still'. That word still means do not make any movement, do not react regardless of what happens. It means no fear, no panic. And you do that only in one place – in the presence of Jesus. The gift of righteousness in Romans 5:17 is a guarantor that we have unhindered access to the Father. So the presence of the Lord is always with us because of what Jesus did for us when he defeated Satan, sin and death. He triumphed over him and made a public embarrassment of him, cancelling every negative condemning word written against us. In doing so, he delivered free of charge, righteousness to anyone who believes, which is a guaranteed presence of Jesus all the time. This is the truth that many religious believers have failed to grasp.

Notice the psalmist says no activity, good or bad, should persuade you to act. The New Living Translation puts it beautifully. It says, *"wait patiently for Him to act"*. A life of rest is a life of "waiting for Jesus to act". But how does that happen, you may ask. Easy. Jesus speaks to us all the time we open His Word. If you don't read or listen to His word, it means you can be passionate but still hear very little from him. Your ability to hear Jesus is measured by the amount of His Word you implement. His Word in you, by the Holy Spirit, will teach you to wait. Let me say this. Jesus opens wombs of the barren. He supplies resources to those in need. Heals the sick. If you can just rest in Him and trust Him in those and other areas, then see Him act. He doesn't want you to prosper through your own efforts.

Remember in the verse above, He says do not worry about 'him who prospereth *in his way.*" God wants to prosper you His way. And His way brings peace and completeness and generosity. The ungodly or self-effort way of prosperity brings turmoil, greed and stinginess or hoarding. God wants to prosper you, but He wants you to be at rest as he guides you to it. That's where the issue is – rest. The story of Joshua reflects exactly what I have described above – resting and waiting for the Lord to act! In this world, they say do something, but in His Word, He says I've done it all, just believe.

The Children of Israel had finally moved into the promised land, the manna had ceased, and they were now going to occupy lands God had promised them, houses they never built and vineyards they never planted. Moses had died and Joshua, the son of Nun was now their leader. The name Joshua is the Hebrew version of the Greek name Jesus. So Joshua is a type of Jesus in the Old Testament. Jericho was the first city to be conquered by Israel in Canaan. News about what God was doing with the Israelites had spread and the inhabitants of Jericho were ready and afraid!

I want you to have this in mind – Israel had never fought a war, no experience whatsoever! The bible says God deliberately took them the way of the desert "in case they face war and turn against Him" because they had never been in battle. Jericho was rich, well supplied at a vantage point in case of war – so everything was against the Israelites. They had only one vantage point – God's grace! Why grace? Because they never applied to have God on their side. They did not deserve or earn His presence. It was out of His lovingkindness that He chose to fight for them. God was on their side. And guess what? That's exactly what Jesus did for you on the cross. He's not only on your side, He's in you and you are in Him. He's not fighting for you, He already conquered, making you more than a conqueror. This is a beautiful life. How could we deserve this kind of love and favour? This affection and warmth. Truly we don't deserve it, it is all by grace. Completely unearned, undeserved! You don't have to be experienced in an area to prevail. Grace makes you attractive. Grace allows Jesus to prevail for you. This truth brings a floodlight of liberty into your spirit and your life can turn around and start having meaning. You can testify too.

> Joshua 6:1-5NIV "Now the gates of Jericho were securely barred because of the Israelites. No one went out and no one came in. 2Then the Lord said to Joshua, "**see, I have delivered Jericho into your hands**, along with its king and its fighting men. 3 March around the city once with all the armed men. Do this for six days. 4Have seven priests carry trumpets of rams' horns in front of the ark. On the seventh day, march around the city seven times, **with the priests blowing the trumpets**. 5When you hear them sound a long blast on the trumpets, have the whole army give a loud shout; then the wall of the city will collapse, and the army will go up, everyone straight in."

Joshua followed to the letter what God said about defeating Jericho. March around the city seven times, and on the seventh day, march seven times and then on the last march, give a shout of victory. Imagine such a simple instruction. But picture the inhabitants of Jericho with an army quietly marching around the city, carrying no weapons and not seemingly wanting to attack. Imagine what was in the minds of the Israelites. What's amazing is that they stood on what God had said, that is to be at rest and wait for the Lord to act. And He did. At the shout, on the last march the city was taken. Rest delivers victory. You need to try this, it works. Rest grows churches, heals relationships, restores wayward children. Rest is life, rest is grace, and His name is Jesus Christ. They walked in the footsteps of their father Abraham who went to war with a handful of people fighting against five kings. He prevailed. Friend, you belong to that breed. You've been cut from that clothe. You possess that nature too. You may not feel it, but you have it

You see, many believers want to live in rest, but they are not patient enough to wait for it. Abraham fell onto the same trap. He believed God, rested on his promise until one day when Sarah was fed up with waiting. She came out of rest and suggested Abraham have a baby with her maidservant. The rest is history, Ishmael was born. But he was not the child of the promise. The child of the promise came at the right time, God's time. At the age of one hundred Abraham had Isaac. He fulfilled his promise. That's why the Bible also says, "at the **right** time, Christ died for the ungodly". He did not come too early or too late, He's always on time. Are you forcing that relationship? Why not be at rest, stop fighting and give in to the Holy Spirit.

You're looking for a job and your resume has been rejected countless times. Your friends bribed their way through very good jobs. Some friends, like Job's friends, tell you to stop this God thing and pay your way in. some spouses, like Job's wife, demand you curse God and die. Painful seasons happen to everyone, just as they happened to our Lord while He was on earth. They come unique to you only, no one understands except the Holy Spirit.

One of the sad questions I get from people I have pastored is what my opinion is on certain issues in their lives. What they don't realise is that the day Jesus lived in my heart was the end of my opinion. What is meant to be my opinion is now Jesus' viewpoint. You see I have the mind of Christ. So when I speak, I speak what Christ would speak. That which is lovely, praiseworthy and pleasant is what I speak, and that is His word. My opinion always fingers the Word of Jesus. Some people have disliked me for that. Others have broken ranks with me because I have fought to speak the mind of Jesus, His word, in response to their needs. Jesus said when they reject you, know that they rejected me first. I speak the mind of Christ because His word brings rest and peace to our souls.

Do like Joshua, who acted on the Word. And the Word of Jesus surely works. As long as you are led by manifestations, rest will not be at work in you. You'll see a low bank balance and you will panic. Get diagnosed with cancer, or probably even get wrongly accused and arrested like Joseph. Many are the ways to lose it but there is only one way to have it - rest – Jesus. Rest is when Jesus runs your life. It is when Jesus takes a turn and you don't question it but follow. It is when the word of God is fully formed in you and Jesus expresses himself in any way. You are God's idea my friend. When you rest, Jesus works. When you work, Jesus rests. The work I'm referring to here is called self-effort. Joshua could have taken an army of strong men, trained them and went into battle, ignoring the Word of the Lord. In both cases, they go to battle. The difference is that the former goes to battle at the instruction of the Lord while the later goes there on their own. See the difference? Resting is then rightly defined as "Jesus working through me". Idleness is not resting, neither is relaxing.

God had given Jericho to Joshua, so Joshua needed to know how to **receive** from an abundant provision of God's Grace – i.e. Be at **rest** knowing that whatever happens, God is in control – **Jesus is our rest** – He says come to me and I will give you rest! Number 6 is the number that represents man, but number 7 signifies completion – rest! God rested because it was **all** Finished. Jesus declared "It is finished" – announcing our entrance into a permanent state of **rest** in him. Blowing of trumpets, as God required of Joshua, became synonymous with the year of Jubilee.

> Leviticus 25:9-11NLT "Then on the Day of Atonement in the fiftieth year, a blow the ram's horn loud and long throughout the land. 10Set this year apart as holy, a time to proclaim freedom throughout the land for all who live there. It will be a jubilee year for you, when each of you may return to the land that belonged to your ancestors and return to your own clan"

Do you notice something? Read it slowly and pay attention. The 50th year was the year after 7 x 7years; the Bible calls it 7 Sabbaths. Every 7th year was a year of REST, both for people, animals and the land. Then the 50th year became the year of Jubilee, a year of release of captives, debt cancellation. And also, the number five represents grace. Friends, it was a year of Grace. We don't enter into Jubilee anymore; He lives in us – His name is Jesus!

> Joshua 6:8-11NIV "When Joshua had spoken to the people, the seven priests carrying the seven trumpets before the Lord went forward, blowing their trumpets, and the ark of the Lord's covenant followed them. 9The armed guard marched ahead of the priests who blew the trumpets, and the rear guard followed the ark. all this time the trumpets were sounding. 10 But Joshua had commanded the army, "Do not give a war cry, do not raise your voices, do not say a word until the day I tell you to shout. Then shout!" 11So he had the ark of the Lord carried around the city, circling it once. then the army returned to camp and spent the night there"

This means that the sounding of horns was a declaration of the year of Jubilee, a declaration of debt cancellation. It was surely a declaration of God's Grace to the children of Israel – they were about to receive what they didn't deserve, Hallelujah. Grace is what was about to happen as they blew the horns. The walls sunk and Joshua took over the city at ease. God fought for him.

Jericho was a city with a strong army of valiant men. It was fortified and they knew they were under siege. God told them to march around the city, blowing trumpets and then **go and rest**. What strategy is that? You're right, anyone would ask that question. Good thing is that I have an answer for it. It's called God's Strategy. The secret is that it works! What's the use of a beautiful design that doesn't work? I would rather settle for God's design that works. They kept declaring God's Grace by sounding the horn – yet nothing seemed to happen. This is where people give up. They ask and say but why is it not working. I have a question for those people. Who said it is not working? Be patient and receive.

My wife's first profession is in the medical field of nursing. She tells me that for antibiotics to work, you have to finish the course! Even if you feel better after taking them for two days, don't stop. If you stop the sickness will pounce on you even stronger. Living a grace-filled life is utilising God's word to the wire, whether there are immediate results or not. Don't stop testifying of what the Lord has done, regardless of the absence of it manifesting.

For the Israelites, after each day – they rested at the camp – no worries. Keep declaring who you are in Christ and **rest**! Do this daily, even if the walls are still glaring at you. – BUT Pastor, how can I say I am rich yet I'm broke? That's where the testimony comes from - declaring and resting. Your testimony won't come quietly, it will announce. You see, when Jesus ascended, He told His disciples to wait – i.e. to be at REST until the Spirit was given. It was exactly on the 50th day after resurrection that there was a trumpet blast of victory from heaven – after 7 sabbaths.

Acts 2:1-2 KJV "and when the day of Pentecost was fully come, they were all with one accord in one place. 2and suddenly there came a sound from heaven as of a rushing mighty wind, and it filled all the house where they were sitting."

Your testimony won't come quietly, it shall be announced on hilltops – he is in you, he wants you to testify! Be at rest and allow him. But you got to **rest** dear, knowing that God is in control! On the last day, the 7th day they blew the war cry trumpet – the walls sunk flat, and the city was taken! Friends, the battle is **not yours**, it belongs to the Lord! The Lord already triumphed more than 2,000 years ago on mount Calvary – You are more than a conqueror, Hallelujah. He made a public spectacle of the devil, taking captivity captive. So, you don't have any battle to fight, except only ONE – Fighting the good fight of faith. What is that Good fight, it is the fight to remain in faith, the fight to remain at rest.

> Hebrews 4:10-11 KJV "For he that is entered into his rest, he also hath ceased from his own works, as god did from his. 11let us **labour therefore to enter into that rest**, lest any man fall after the same example of unbelief."

I believe as you read along, the life of Jesus spreads mightily into your being that you may fully trust Him and let him run your life, which is entering His rest.

13 | Eternally Secure in Christ

One of the key things in a love relationship is the aspect of security. A wife may receive all the expensive gifts her husband can buy her but when she is not sure about her position as the only wife, that affects her attitude towards her husband and everything she does. Everything comes with a "what if"! What if he divorces me; what if he has another wife or what if he just leaves me? Insecurity is bad, it keeps you in prison. Insecurity is one big source of unrest in believers. That source of insecurity is wrong information being given to them on a regular basis. Many believers are not sure if God really loves them. Many are also not sure of their destiny after they die regardless of how much they love the Lord. They are not sure because they are very insecure because of what they know.

I know of a musician who ministered powerfully and loved the Lord so much. Unfortunately, he contracted HIV/AIDS. At the time, the stigma of this disease was so bad you were considered an outcast, a sinful person, seen as immoral etc. This musician lived the final years of his life in great condemnation. He even composed a song, which was one of his last if not his last, with lyrics saying,

"I'm afraid of hell fire". You see immorality is sin, and sin is bad. Whether under the Law or Grace sin is sin and is bad. It wrecks families, destroys relationships and steals all the joy you may have. Sin is bad.

The Law that was given by Moses and Grace that came by Jesus Christ agree that sin is very bad and must be punished for. The major difference between the two is how sin is effectively and completely dealt with. The Law of Moses demands the use of your strength in keeping every letter of the Law, failure to which you are as guilty as breaking all, yet grace defeats sin by our faith in Jesus. James 2:10 NLT says, "For the person who keeps all of the laws except one is as guilty as a person who has broken all of God's laws." So, this musician was not secure in God's grace, rather he remained deeply in condemnation of which, instead of running to the Lord to depend on His strength regarding that weakness, he focussed on his ability to save himself and there was no hope. He died a broken man.

Many believers are like this musician. They are not sure of the security of their salvation. They are always in repentance mode in case they die without repenting of their past sin. You notice something, they are always conscious about "not" sinning or "not" falling into sin, so they will sin even more and repent even more! It's like getting a job and be told you are on three months' probation. Those three months become the hardest because if you are not good enough you will lose your employment. Your performance plays a major role in the security of your employment, right? Yet after probation, and you are declared a permanent employee, you feel great about yourself and usually your performance improves drastically knowing your employment is secure. While this has been entrenched in us and is true with man, it is not so with Jesus. God did not set up salvation that way. When you receive eternal life, God does not put you on probation to see how good you are, no ways! Jesus secured our redemption forever, once and for all (Hebrews 9:12). That verse is key, it is supposed to bring rest to your soul knowing that beyond the grave you have assurance and security that you will be with the Lord forever.

Jesus gave us eternal security as a gift. Instead of using the Law for defeating sin, Romans 6:14 ESV says, "For sin will have no dominion over you, since you are not under law but under grace". Again, a life of grace is a life of depending on Jesus. How do we do that? We do this by keeping our eyes on Jesus, the champion who initiates and perfects our faith (Hebrews 12:2). All the perfection of our faith is done by Jesus when we are constantly focussed on Him. Hebrews 3:1 goes on to say "Therefore, holy brothers and sisters, who share in the heavenly calling, fix your thoughts on Jesus, whom we acknowledge as our apostle and high priest." A life of grace, which is a life of rest, is a life of fixation on the Lord Jesus. As a man thinks, so is he (Proverbs 23:7).

We become conscious of Him only and not us; on His performance not on ours, good or bad. Take it simple like this. If you change the way you think, your actions will change. It's all domiciled in thinking. Deal with thoughts, you deal with fornication, murders, gossip, lies, etc. In 1

Corinthians 2:16, the apostle Paul makes a big declaration. He says, by God's Spirit "For, "Who can know the LORD's thoughts? Who knows enough to teach him?" But we understand these things, **for we have the mind of Christ**". Hallelujah! Grace uses the mind of Jesus to think resulting in the same behaviour as Jesus. The law lets you use your own mind and strength to accomplish the impossible.

This is glorious. Jesus did not just die for our past sins and leave us to battle it out with our present and future challenges and see how to redeem ourselves. No, He didn't do that. He redeemed us from our past, present and future sins. After that, He gave us His divine nature. He also gave us his mind, so that we can think like Him so that we can behave like Him. Philippians 2:5NIV says "In your relationships with one another, have **the same mindset as Christ Jesus**".

You see, grace has made available the mind of Christ for us to use. We have a choice to use it in our relationships and everything else in life. We do this by reading or studying the scriptures, listening to inspired teachings and eventually living according to those teachings. Unbelievers do not have this option unless they accept Jesus as their Lord and saviour. This gives you rest knowing that you are eternally secure. There is no sin too big for you because Jesus defeated the mother of all sins, Sin itself. That nature was defeated. This truth liberates you to know that you are not only free, but you are everything that Jesus Christ is. His life is active in you, living your life for you as you allow Him to. This is rest.

1 John 4:17NIV says "This is how love is made complete among us so that we will have **confidence on the day of judgment**: In this world, we are like Jesus". Ok, this verse may sound incomplete without verse 13 which says "And so we **know** and **rely on the love God has for us**. God is love. Whoever lives in love lives in God, and God in them." Wow! This is incredible. You see that. We rely on the love of God. A life of rest is so secure eternally that its only reliance is in the love of God, and not your own love.

Man's love is insincere at its best, it changes circumstantially. God's love is different! It has no moods. It is consistent. And because of our knowledge and reliance on the love of God, we have confidence on the day of judgment! Come on, did you hear that? The only way you can be confident going to judgment is knowing fully that you are not guilty. All your wrongs have been forgiven, and the judge has you covered. That's exactly what Christ has done for us. The last part of verse 17 says 'in this world, we are like Jesus'. Friends, if I start thinking like you, I will act like you and before long people around us will be like, mhhhh Sbanga is like so and so. Because they see my actions exactly like yours. Wonderful! Let's take this further.

A parent, who wants their child to behave like the child next door would rant and tell their child "be like John next door, can't you see how he behaves?" I can guarantee you, that child will be worse. Why? The problem is not with the child, it's with the parent. The parent needs to know inside information on how the other parent has established a thought pattern that produces such good results. Then, in turn, proceed to establish such thinking which will eventually become a behaviour. I bet you agree with me on this. I'll stretch it further. Bad sinful behaviour can never be stopped by us ranting at God's people to stop doing bad things. But it can be stopped when they start using the mind of Jesus for their own thinking. Fixation on Jesus says it all.

Christ consciousness and knowing you are eternally secure in Him is fundamental in living a restful glorious life. Ever noticed some believers move from revival to revival looking for something? When an evangelist comes to town, they follow him until another "more powerful" one surfaces. They move from church to church searching for something they can't find. The first few months they may enjoy the love and goodness of brethren, but soon will see certain things they don't like, and they will leave. All that borders on insecurity.

Insecurity is a result of wrong information. Wrong information comes from a wrong interpretation of literature, in this case, the Bible. God wants you to know that you are dearly loved. And He has given you all the love you need to love all those who are around you. He wants you to live in His love and know who you are in Him, that you are like Him in this world. He wants you to know that when you die today your place in His kingdom is guaranteed and secure. He wants you to know that sin has no power over you because you are under grace not under the law. He wants you to be aware that you can live a purely healthy life because He is healthy. As He is so are we.

Because He is prosperous, so are you. Because He is forgiving, so are you when people wrong you. He is generous, so are you!

This is Good News. Jesus is very attractive. In Him we have health, wealth, life, wisdom, peace, joy, patience, righteousness, you name it. My knowledge of these things is too wonderful. By the way He also says in Romans 10:13NIV "Love does no harm to a neighbour. Therefore, love is the fulfilment of the law." And this is after Jesus says in John 13:34NIV "A new command I give you: Love one another. As I have loved you, so you must love one another." That love He wants us to use to each other, He has given it to us. Because we live in Him, in His love, He also lives in us and we radiate His person mightily to everyone around us. Our constant awareness of Him shields us from all sin and develops godly manifestations which are pleasing to the Lord.

14 | GRACE, REST AND HOLINESS

If you receive God's abundant grace and His gift of righteousness (Romans 5:17), you'll find rest in Him. In Jeremiah 6:16 KJV the Bible says "...ask for the old paths, where *is* the **good way**, and **walk therein,** and ye shall **find rest** for your souls..." True rest comes when you walk in that "good way". And Jesus clearly tells us who that "good way" is in John 14:6 NIV - "Jesus answered, **"I am the way** and the truth and the life. No one comes to the Father except through me". That "good way" Jeremiah spoke about is none other than Jesus Himself, Hallelujah! Again, Jesus would say, in Matthew 11:29 NIV "Take my yoke upon you and learn from me, for I am gentle and humble in heart, and you will **find rest** for your souls." Friends, rest can only manifest in your life if you walk in that "good way" - Jesus, or rather let Jesus walk your life. And walking with Jesus means receiving His offer of grace and the gift of righteousness. This means giving up your life and let Him live it for you (Galatians 2:20). That's the difference between a believer who confesses all the truths about grace and the one who lives in those truths. The latter walks in complete grace and is at rest, thus naturally produces the fruit of the Spirit, leading to holiness. It's that simple. A life of rest is a life preoccupied about the Father's love that the presence of sin is unnoticed. Rest, in grace, makes you live effortless holiness. This is wonderful.

Once you are rested in Him it means that you can now let Him run your life. I have a question for you. What kind of a lifestyle do you think Jesus would live? A life of holiness, right? Correct. Jesus makes us holy because He lives in us by faith. A grace-filled life is a life full of God. It is impossible to do sin naturally. **Romans 6:6NLT** says "We know that our old sinful selves were crucified with Christ so that sin might lose its power in our lives. We are ***no longer slaves to sin***." You can sin by choice, but you are not a slave to it. Slaves do things they may not want to do.

Sinning by choice saddens God because there is no more other sacrifice for sins except that which Jesus has already done (Hebrews 10:26). God never takes away man's will when they are saved. Unbelievers or sinners are oppressed with a nature that makes them sin unwillingly. They are restless. They may do some good righteous things, but you can't trust them to continue doing right in every area of their lives. You can domesticate a snake, but you can never take away its nature. So is a lion or a dog. Some domesticated dogs have turned and mauled their owners. But why? You did everything to keep it good. Yes, the issue is simple. It still overflows with its nature. Jesus described this condition perfectly describing the Pharisees in John 8:43-44 NLT

> 42 Jesus told them, "If God were your Father, you would love me, because I have come to you from God. I am not here on my own, but

he sent me. 43 Why can't you understand what I am saying? It's because you can't even hear me! 44 For you are the children of your father the devil, and you love to do the evil things he does. He was a murderer from the beginning. He has always hated the truth, because there is no truth in him. When he lies, it is consistent with his character; for he is a liar and the father of lies.

Notice something? He says if God were your Father, you would **love**. Why? Because children carry the DNA of their father. The nature of the father is seen in the sons or vice versa. In contrast, Jesus calls them the "children of your father the devil". This sounds very strong yet so true because they "love to do the evil things he (the devil) does". Jesus says, when the devil lies, "it is consistent with his character". When an unbeliever does unrighteous things, it is consistent with their nature.

Satan, in his deceitful lies, has misrepresented sin and made it look attractive. Today's blockbuster movies and music promote violence, immorality, nakedness and horror. Sin is very bad. It wrecks families. It destroys relationships. It might have momentary pleasures (Hebrews 11:25), yet in reality, sin is very bad. There is nothing attractive at all in sin. The consequences are obvious; suicides, murders and the like are the norm in our society today. Look at the news any day. What the world calls news is nothing other than the glorification of the bad effects of sin. Headlines are always about war, murders, financial crisis, how things will get worse and so on. Such news sells, so they say. Friends, this deceit goes a long way, deceiving even believers to think that Christ in them is a loss of joy, which is not true. Jesus calls him the father of all lies, who lied from the beginning.

In Christ, we have the beautiful nature to naturally produce love, joy, peace, forbearance, kindness, goodness, faithfulness, gentleness and self-control (Gal. 5:22-23). This is called the fruit of the Spirit. Note that it is the fruit **of the Spirit, not your fruit**. You don't produce all those good deeds, the Spirit does. What has religion done? It has poured all that burden to produce such fruit on you the person. You try hard and fail even harder. Instead of enjoying and growing in the love relationship and fellowship with the Father, by the Holy Spirit, you are enduring the pain of always repenting because you always do wrong. You are not producing the fruit. You just don't seem to be producing the right fruit.

You may ask, but pastor, how is that possible when I have the nature of Christ? Easy answer. Wrong believing will always result in wrong behaviour although it does not take away your nature. Religious believers are not required to be born again! No ways. Because being born again, you receive the nature of Christ. How you believe after that is key to an effortless life of freedom. The apostle Paul said to Timothy "take heed to your doctrine". He wanted him to pay close attention to his teachings. That which was meant to give life could quickly be a source of grief. God's standard of righteousness is impossible without depending totally on Him. Again, he says that our "self-effort" righteousness (not sin, imagine – but righteousness) is like filthy rags. A life of holiness is very easy when grace is in control of every aspect of our beings. Where there is grace, there is rest.

The Lord told me something the other day. He said if you take away the letter G from Grace you remain with the word "Race". When you take God off your life, you don't walk in grace anymore, you're in a race. You judge people not based on Christ in them but their natural abilities or disabilities. The apostle Paul, who was a champion of grace and rest in Christ, had this to say in 2 Corinthians 5:16NLT "So we have stopped evaluating others from a human point of view. At one time, we thought of Christ merely from a human point of view. How differently we know him now!" Walk into a church today and see how believers segregate themselves based on skin colour, place of origin or even the more common one, financial status. Sit down and listen to the teaching then you understand why. It's mainly condemnation and self-effort, regarding one another on a human point of view.

I served in a church that loved God so much and had experienced a revival and phenomenal growth. The teachings promoted words like "keep pushing", "be strong like so and so" etc. Naturally, that sounds great. I was a naturally strong-willed person, so I pushed and pushed and pushed. So were my fellow believers. Until one day, when I was in London visiting a beautiful church there when the Lord said to me "You are trying too hard. I want you to change your message. Start teaching grace, love and my glory". At that point, I was worn out. I had come to the end of myself. I needed help, a saviour. Previously I had asked my pastor what I needed to do for the church to grow. I had poured out all my youth to the church, my resources, branded the church but still couldn't go beyond a certain number. Why a certain number? Because our success was based on the number of people we had won, not necessarily on the truth that we are a success with or without numbers. My pastor's response was "I don't know Sbanga, just keep pushing". That did little to encourage me. I knew my ability to push had been exhausted. I had come to the very end of myself, yet I didn't know it as I do now. Until God said, "change your message".

John the Baptist was a great success even though he was beheaded (Mark 6), dying young in his early thirties. He was a great success though his disciples left him to follow Jesus (John 1:35-37). Jesus, commenting about John, who was a prophet in the old covenant said in Luke 7:28NIV "I tell you, among those born of women there is **no one greater than John**..." This is too much. A man who lived only three decades, never married, lost disciples, was a lone ranger preaching from the wilderness, got beheaded and you call such a man the greatest? You gonna be kidding some may say. You see, success is never measured by human standards, but God's. Anna, the widow who was married for seven years, lost her husband and never married would be considered a failure in today's success measurement. But Anna fulfilled her prophetic mandate to intercede for the ministry and appearing of Jesus. Luke 2:36-37 says of Anna when Jesus was born - "36Anna, **a prophet**, was also there in the Temple.

She was the daughter of Phanuel from the tribe of Asher, and she was very old. Her husband died when they had been married only seven years. 37Then she lived as a widow to the age of eighty-four. **She never left the Temple** but stayed there day and night, **worshipping God with fasting and prayer**." A life of rest is not a life in competition with others. It's a life that is totally sufficient with Jesus. That's the New Covenant life Jesus purchased with his own blood.

After the Lord had spoken to me about changing my message, my wife and I decided to research about the love of God. The closest I could get to was a brother, many years prior, who told me that his favourite topic is the love of God. When we discovered these truths about God's grace, I honestly thought I was the only one with that revelation in the world. It was epic. Life transforming. I was glued to the scriptures. I went through the scriptures by myself, verse by verse and it was like a floodlight, glowing in my spirit. I understood everything in great simplicity.

The message was too good to be true. I discovered how practical Jesus wants to run our lives for our benefit. I was like a child with candy, you can't take it away from me. I got it finally. Later on, I discovered there are many pastors all over the world, who have been labouring to teach these truths. Many of them with small probably despised churches, while some have large churches. The message is the same. Friends, I pray this book does the same to you. My life continues to be at rest in Jesus. I worry not because He cares for me. I'm free. Nothing moves me. The apostle Paul was so much at rest and understood the New Covenant that he said in Acts 20:24 KJV "But **none**

of these things move me, neither count I my life dear unto myself, so that I might finish my course with joy, and the ministry, which I have received of the Lord Jesus, to testify the **gospel of the grace of God**." He arrived at that point where nothing had the ability to move or persuade him otherwise. His mandate was none other than to "testify the gospel of the grace of God".

This was the gospel I needed to hear when I had come to the end of myself. The gospel of the grace of God. This gospel is truly Good News. Simply put, it says Jesus has done it for me, I need to depend on His finished work of the cross and not my effort. He finished so I can rest, no stress. His grace brought rest for my soul. Rest can never come without grace. Grace takes you to accept that you can't. if you can accept that, then you can rest knowing that He can. This is the beginning of an effortless holy life.

My wife was talking to one lady at church telling her how she kept confessing that she was healed of her tummy problem. The lady asked her if she got healed. In hindsight, she said she didn't know. And guess what, the other lady, (I believe by the Spirit) said 'mhhh pastor, if you haven't had that problem then it means you were healed'. And how true was that? I also realised; ah she hasn't complained for months. Surely, she was healed. You see, grace makes you confess the word of God that says you are already healed, blessed etc. even though there is no visual evidence of it. And that puts you at rest because you know God can not lie. That life of rest then brings eternal peace and the manifestation then comes at times without you realising it.

15 | REST IN GOD'S LOVE

God made life under the New Covenant far much better than it was in the old. In the Old Covenant of the Law of Moses, you needed to keep all the commandments to be worth receiving the blessing. You had to be worth to receive. Failing to keep one out of more than six hundred of those laws meant that you had broken all, whether you were aware of it or not (James 2:10). This was serious. Deuteronomy 28 made things even worse by promising a curse to everyone who didn't keep the law to the letter. Verse 15 says "However, if you do not obey the Lord your God and do not *carefully follow all* his commands and decrees I am giving you today, all these curses will come on you and overtake you:" Wow, see that? You had to carefully follow ALL, not some. Breaking one was as good as breaking all. The curses pronounced are very harsh. Read that whole chapter. In addition to poverty, those curses included death, disease, pain, emotional breakdowns, mental sickness and the like. God, in His abundant love and mercy, sent His son Jesus to redeem us from the curse of the law. Let me show you the verse.

Galatians 3:13NLT says "But Christ has rescued us from the curse **pronounced by the law**. When he was hung on the cross, **he took upon himself the curse** for our wrongdoing. For it is written in the Scriptures, "Cursed is everyone who is hung on a tree." Other versions use the word redemption. The love of God came to rescue us from the bondage of the curse that came with failure to keep the law by taking our position and the punishment due to us. He rescued us from the curse of the law. How did He do that? Galatians 5:14NIV answers that. You will love this verse. It says: "For the *entire law* is fulfilled in keeping this one command: "Love your neighbour as yourself" Glory to God. So, by simple loving other people, the New Covenant says you have kept the entire law! Just one command, of love.

I love Jesus. You may ask and say, pastor, it's difficult to love my neighbour as myself. You are right. It's impossible if you use your own strength. That's where grace and rest come in. What Jesus was simply saying, and eventually Paul, was that you cannot use your personal ability to love other people. Personal ability or effort has an elastic limit, yet God's ability is limitless. The only way to love your neighbour as you love yourself is for you to allow the ability of Jesus to be at work in you. A life of rest is the life of the spirit. Verse 18 of Galatians 5 says "But if you are led by the Spirit, you are not under the law". Walking in the Spirit is walking in love. The most spiritual people can be seen by the dimension they express real love to other people. It is because their actions reveal what has happened in their hearts. Their actions of love come out naturally, not pre-meditated. The biggest problem in the body of Christ is that priority has been given in building big church buildings with big numbers at the expense of building believers to have Christ fully formed in them to the extent that His character can naturally influence day to day life. The love of Christ needs to be fully formed in us.

Romans 5:5NLT says "And this hope will not lead to disappointment. For we know how dearly God loves us because he has **given us** the Holy Spirit **to fill our hearts with his love**" Hallelujah! He has given us totally for free, unearned, undeserved and surely His unmerited precious Holy Spirit. And His purpose was to fill our hearts with the love of God. Friends, God does not expect you to love using your love, no. He has given you all the necessary tools to love – His very own love. You can love the way God loves because you have His love in you. The problem is that you don't believe that because you were taught wrongly. The love of God is in you because the Holy Spirit has filled your heart with His love.

You may say, but pastor, I don't feel it. I must feel it to believe it is there! That's exactly where the problem is. You want to believe after feeling like Thomas the disciple. He said in John 20:25NLT "**I won't believe it** unless I see the nail wounds in his hands, put my fingers into them, and place my hand into the wound in his side". Believers have everything they need in them but do not believe they do. So failure to live in rest is aa belief problem. God's approach is different. He says in Mark 11:24NIV "I tell you, you can pray for anything, and if you believe that you've received it, it will be yours". The emphasis is that you believe you have it then you will have it. Belief comes first before manifestation. So is the love of God in you. You should believe that the Holy Spirit in you has surely poured out the love of God in you as the scriptures say. Standing on that firm belief, don't let anything move you and you will see the love of God manifesting mightily in you. Wrong believing can keep you in unrest for the rest of your life while right believing can liberate you into a life of constant fulfilment.

When Adam sinned in the garden, do you remember what happened? Religion has taught us that when we sin, God is after us to punish and finish us off. And this position is picked up from the scriptures and wrongly applied or interpreted. But, using the law of first mention, let's see what happened when man first sinned. Adam disobeyed God. After they had sinned, and their eyes opened **Genesis 3:8-10NLT** gives us God's response. Read this slowly and understand.

> "When the cool evening breezes were blowing, the man and his wife heard **the LORD God walking** about in the garden. So, they hid from the LORD God among the trees. 9Then the **Lord God called to the man, "Where are you**?" 10He replied, "I heard you walking in the garden, so I hid. I was afraid because I was naked."

This is amazing. Man sins and God responds by coming to look for him. Do you see that? And that has never changed. God has been looking for man ever since to save him from sin. In John 15:16NLT Jesus affirms this by saying "You didn't choose me. I chose you. I appointed you to go and produce lasting fruit, so that the Father will give you whatever you ask for, using my name". In your worst state, God is out looking for you. Why, because He loves you. He looked for Adam, found him and took away his embarrassment by covering him. God sent Jesus; we didn't look for Him, but he looked for us. By His blood, He cleansed us of all sin. By the water of His water, we are constantly cleansed daily (John 15:3, Galatians 5:26).

Why am I sharing this? How is it related to rest? Satan has lied to man and told them that God doesn't love them and wants to take their life, money, their luxury and their peace. While many people confess God loves them, they don't believe that. When a problem strikes, they seek answers everywhere except from God or in the house of the Lord. As a pastor, I have noted a trend. When things go tough, believers stop coming to church.

One believer said to me "pastor, I will come to church when I sort my things out". And many have said that. You ask why? It's because while they know God loves them, they don't believe He does to the extent He wants to carry their burdens. So, they are happy with God when they don't have burdens. When burdens come, they use human effort. When they fail, they blame God for not helping them. This is important. The life of rest begins with the assurance that God loves you. That assurance, firm and clear should be in your heart all the time. That affirmation should be beyond any reasonable doubt. Whether good or bad happens to us, we should be so much at peace in God's love. Jesus knew His Father loved Him. God loves you, my friend. You need to believe that. He loves you so much that He gave us Jesus.

When Adam sinned, God came looking for him. When Cain murdered his brother, guess who showed up? God. Jesus came from heaven to earth, we did not send a delegation to heaven to request a saviour, no! God did not stop sending water, warmth, harvest, etc on earth because Adam sinned. He remains our supply because His love has no end. Never doubt the love of God.

I attempted suicide twice in my life. In both instances, I felt a vacuum in my heart, deep emptiness. I didn't feel loved. I can't remember the exact ages, but I was between 7 and probably 10 years old. The devil wanted to kill me young. I used to cry a lot alone. I didn't love my life. I wouldn't think anyone could have done anything to help. I remember clearly, walking into 'our' bedroom, preparing a noose, climbing up to the roof securing it. I didn't know God then and was just religious. So I locked the door, climbed the chair, put the noose on my neck. Just before kicking that chair, a voice spoke to me and said "don't! Give me a chance, I love you". This voice was different, it melted all the pain in my heart. I cried and took the noose off my neck, off the roof truss and put it away. No one knew about this.

The second time, we were playing outside our home as children and I thought this was it. I stood by the gate, looked at oncoming traffic and identified a car that would kill me. When the car was about 20m away, I ran right in front of it. The driver applied his brakes and the car stopped right after hitting my legs. I fell, but I wasn't hurt, just a slight bruise. I wanted to die. My mum was angry at me obviously, but she didn't know I wanted to die. That's why when Jesus came into my heart when I was about sixteen, no one could dissuade me otherwise. I couldn't believe the miracle that Christ was now living in me. I have heard of many people in the same situation, if only they could give Jesus a chance. Their lives would never be the same.

Growing in the church was very good but it had its own let down, emphasis on behaviour than a heart change from within. This is called religion; trying to live a Christian life using self-effort. When religion crept in and crowded my relationship with God, deep in my heart I longed for that pure experiential love of God. Religion put a burden in me, using self-effort to produce the love that only God can give. That's why when God rekindled the enlightenment about His love, grace and glory nothing could stop me. It was my life. It is my life.

The love of God is my life. Everyone needs to know God loves them. More-so that He cares for every aspect of their lives. This is foundational. Before demonstrating power and miracles, prophecies and gifts of the Spirit, which are all beneficial, you need to experience the love of God in your heart and be affirmed that "He will never leave you nor forsake you" (Hebrews 13:5) as a literal position not a religious statement. This knowledge is foundational in living a life of rest. You see this is personal. No church, no organisation, no prophet or pastor, no husband or wife, nobody but you and God. That personal intimacy and affirmation that God loves you. This is extremely important. All these other things, people and organisations come and go, but God is the same yesterday, today and forever (Hebrews 13:8). That personal affirmation of God's love in your heart makes you rest and fully trust in Him. Jesus did not come for a group of people; he came for you. He came for me. In fact, he personalises his love to you. That knowledge is powerful. It will usher divine rest into your soul.

Rest is that secure place of the love of God. Once you are secure in His goodness and love then you cannot be religiously manipulated. At this point, I'll ask you a question. Do you know the love of God? Don't be quick to answer. Probably you received Jesus, you serve in the church and do many activities, but deep in your heart do you truly have a vibrant love relationship and fellowship with Jesus? If not, I want to help you. Go into your room or quiet place and prepare to pray. Before you do that; I have one assurance for you, that God will hear your prayer and a miracle of the love of God will take place in your heart, you'll feel His love.

In Matthew 6:6NLT Jesus said "But when you pray, go away by yourself, shut the door behind you, and pray to your Father in private. Then your Father, who sees everything, will reward you." So, there is a definite reward for you today. And I pray that it be a miraculous outpour of the experiential love of God into your heart by the Holy Spirit. Don't be in haste as you pray. Talk to him like you are talking to someone you know. Once you are ready, begin to pray. In your prayer include these words as a guide:

"Heavenly Father, I know you love me. Thank you for your love. Help me experience your love in my heart right now and all the days of my life. I know you are listening to me. I want to be constantly conscious that you love me. In Jesus' precious name, amen"

From now on constantly confess that you are "God's beloved". You don't have to feel it to confess it. But when you constantly confess it, you'll be amazed at what would have happened in the next few weeks. That experiential love of Jesus will be all over your spirit, soul and body. All the challenges you have will seem like simple obstacles. You'll sleep better, plan better and be more content with whom you are and what you have. My friend, this is the beginning of rest. I live a rested life. Nothing moves me. Anyone's opinion about me doesn't matter. And I don't use my effort at all. Those opinions mean nothing to me.

What matters is what Jesus thinks about me. And He says through Jeremiah 29:11 KJV "For I know the thoughts that I think toward you, saith the LORD, **thoughts of peace**, and not of evil, to give you an expected end." So, Jesus thinks of peace and not disaster, when He thinks of me. I will hold on to that opinion. And that's what you need too. I will repeat it, that's what you need too. Knowing that God thinks good things concerning you. That gives you peace and rest knowing that He is in charge. He's not out to get you. Some people know God as a "hell sender". No, God is love. That's who He is. Hell is real. The lake of fire is real. It wasn't made for you, though. It was made for the devil and his angels (Matthew 25:41), never for you. Never! People will go there because they reject Jesus and his solution to sin. They go on to accept Satan's deception and lies that sin is good. God punishes all sin. And guess what? All your sin was punished on the body of Jesus. That's why all your guilt is absolved because of what Jesus has already done for you. A life of grace, a life of rest is a life that accepts the fulness of what Jesus did on the cross. What a life this is! Glory to Jesus.

The woman caught in the very act of adultery by the Pharisees was in fear and condemnation for she knew her fate, but when she was thrown to Jesus, who overflows with the love of the Father, forgiveness came. The law rightly demanded her condemnation and death (Lev. 20:10), but grace offered her acceptance and life (John 10:10). 2 Corinthians 3:6NLT says "He has enabled us to be ministers of his New Covenant. This is a covenant not of written laws, but of the Spirit. The old written covenant ends in death; but under the New Covenant, the Spirit gives life."

The preaching of the law never gives life, no matter how perfect and holy the law is. It never gives acceptance and life but ends in death. The New Covenant is the covenant of the grace of God that overflows in God's love and acceptance. It is a covenant that focusses on Jesus and not you. It is a covenant that guarantees your acceptance – righteousness – so that you can boldly worship God and live your life without fear. This woman caught in adultery was a beneficiary of the grace of God, and that grace is available today, right now as you read this. Hope is here.

You can't forgive unless you love. God never turns away anyone who needs His love, never! He has an oversupply and will never run dry. Regardless of what you have done, Jesus is always welcoming, embracing and loving. Saul of Tarsus had murdered believers including Stephen (Acts 22:20) and yet the love of God reached Him. He preached the grace of God with a passion. He lived a fulfilling life of trusting in God. That's what a life of rest is all about. The apostle Peter denied Jesus three times, yet when Jesus resurrected, he specifically reached out to Peter. He said in Mark 16:7NIV "But go, tell his disciples **and Peter**, 'He is going ahead of you into Galilee. There you will see him, just as he told you.'" Jesus knew that he could be feeling condemned, so he reached out to him by his love.

The love of God is wonderful. His love never carries condemnation. What have you done? Are you a murderer like Saul? Or sexually immoral like the woman caught in the act of adultery? Or a money launderer like Zacchaeus the tax collector? With all these, Jesus embraced and overflowed them with his love. You qualify for his love too because of His grace. Maybe you are a believer and have done the above, walked away from God. Friend, if God could accept sinners in such extreme situations, would he honestly not welcome you and love you? He does! Luke 15 tells us about the prodigal son who was welcomed back regardless of squandering all his inheritance. His father did not ask many questions, He just embraced him. God still loves and welcomes you.

I will wrap up this chapter with the story of the Good Samaritan. Just to show you how much God loves you. An expert of the law had asked Jesus how he could inherit eternal life. Jesus pointed Him towards the law (because Jesus had not yet died). One of the laws he highlighted was to "love your neighbour as you love yourself". Because this expert of the law wanted to justify himself, he had asked Jesus who his neighbour was (Luke 10:29). It was at this point that Jesus told him the parable of the good Samaritan. A man, a Jew, coming from worshipping in Jerusalem, was beaten up by robbers and left for dead. A priest (a Jew) and a Levite (a Jew too) pass by and they do not help this dying man because the Law of Moses did not allow them to touch dead bodies else they would be unclean.

Leviticus 21 outlines these rules clearly. Verse 1 (KJV) says, for example, "And the LORD said unto Moses, speak unto the priests the sons of Aaron, and say unto them, there shall none be defiled for the dead among his people". Verse 11 (NLT) stretches this requirement and says, concerning the priesthood "He must not defile himself by **going near** a dead body. He may not make himself ceremonially unclean even for his father or mother." This was true for all Levites. Levites were a tribe of priests for they served in the temple. Touching or going near a dead body, according to the Law was unacceptable for the priesthood. In the story of the Good Samaritan, the priest and Levite rightly couldn't help this "dead man" because the Law prohibited them.

Notice this: the near-dead victim was a Jew. Fellow Jews couldn't help him because the Law had a restriction. Jesus then stretches the story introducing a Samaritan, who quickly helps this man by supplying him with all he needed, paying over and above all the bill requirements He could incur. As a Samaritan, he couldn't help a Jew because Jews had no dealings with Samaritans (John 4:9). All this Jew-Samaritan animosity dated back when Israel was invaded by Assyria and intermarriage produced a nation of half-Jews half-Assyrians called Samaritans. This Samaritan, aware of all this decided to go against it, and let compassion and love have the better of the day. This Samaritan was a true neighbour. This parable was a picture of law versus grace. The law restricts you from doing good, even if your heart so desires to. You fear the consequences of doing good. You are restless. What if rings in your mind. Yet grace is a total opposite, it offers that which is not deserved. The 'near dead' Jew did not deserve any help from the Samaritan, yet the Samaritan still gave him that help. He didn't ask any questions why and how he got himself in that situation, but simply helped the man.

This story is about Jesus, pictured as the good Samaritan! He came to a world that did not deserve salvation and died for it. He supplied all that man needed by dying on the cross securing our redemption forever. He didn't ask any questions why and how we found ourselves in depression, sin, anger etc. no, He simply said "whosoever shall believe in Him shall not perish but have everlasting life" because "God so loved the world" (John 3:16). Jesus was telling this expert of the law that for him to inherit eternal life, he needed to embrace the new life of grace that enables you to do what the Samaritan did. Only through Jesus can that be possible. That man who was helped by the Samaritan rested knowing that all his bills were fully paid. Exactly this is how God wants us to rest. He wants you and me to be so much at rest knowing that Jesus has paid fully the price of our redemption, and we did not pay for it, it is the gift of God (Ephesians 2:8). A life of rest does not discriminate based on skin colour, race, lineage or language (Galatians 3:28, Colossians 3:11). A life of rest sees everyone through the lenses of grace. The lenses of grace see the love of God in everyone.

Sadly, out there are people preaching hate, separation, condemnation and curses. God's people are in prison of the fear of men. Prophets and miracle workers are feared for their powers, and many have manipulated their gifts to subdue God's people. This can't be further from the truth. Whatever it is they teach; it is not the good news. It may be exciting news to many, but not good news. Good News of Jesus Christ liberates, gives hope and keeps you in love. Jude 1:21 says "keep yourselves in God's love as you wait for the mercy of our Lord Jesus Christ to bring you to eternal life." 1 Corinthians 13 affirms that no matter what your abilities are "but do not have love, (you are) nothing". You remain nothing without love, yet you are everything with it. And God is that love. 1 Corinthians 14:1 says "Let love be your highest goal!" Other versions would say earnestly pursue love. Friends, the gospel is never good news outside the emphasis of God's love.

16 | STOP TRYING, REST

I was summoned into an SUV by two respected men of God with a respected following. I needed counselling and I was hurting at the time. Life was tough. I couldn't afford a shirt or even a decent pair of pants. During a wedding of one of the church members, I decided to take advantage of that opportunity to receive counsel and guidance. The two men of God summoned me to their SUV parked outside. I got in and shared with them my issues. When it was time for them to respond, I was in for the unexpected. The conversation turned against me. They began to condemn me for not dressing "like a pastor". My looks and presentation did not portray a pastor. A lot went through my mind as my thoughts raced on what a pastor looked like. Was there a biblical requirement for a pastors' dressing? I looked at these successful pastors. They resembled CEOs, clad in expensive suits and their cars were good. They lived in affluent suburbs. This was the total opposite of me. I was poor, I lived in a poor suburb and hardly could afford anything pretty at the time. I left that car worse off than I had walked in.

Because I didn't know any better, and there was no alternative, I started trying hard to "look like a pastor". I tried very hard to fit in the mould of a pastor "as expected". I borrowed pants, ties and shirts when attending meetings or going to minister. I shared suits and shoes with fellow friends. As my financial situation improved, so I started looking more like a pastor. This was hard and quite oppressive. I believe the people I pastored were also under the same pressure to look "right". I was restless though I didn't know it. I loved God, but I was restless. I worked hard for Jesus, but I was restless. I gave all to advance the kingdom, my time my resources, but honestly, I was restless. The message I believed did not help.

My passion and selflessness in my service were not enough to bring in that peace and rest in my soul. I kept trying and I kept failing. How come even the fruit of the Spirit was hard to come by. How true was the Bible? I arrived at a place called the end of myself. I needed a saviour, yet I was a Christian, I was a pastor. I couldn't measure up to a church standard, neither could I get to a pastoral standard. There had to be a standard where your effort never counts. Where pleasing a man was not a prerequisite to peace and living a life free of curses, condemnation and accusations. A life where inner peace and security can't be traded for anything else. A life where inner success and rest is more valuable than external success. I'm talking of a life that Jesus Christ intended.

My friends, it was when Jesus brought into my heart this revelation of His love and grace. That revelation where righteousness is truly given to me as a gift, I didn't need to attain it. I was convinced I was the only one with that understanding of the scriptures. I consumed the scriptures like a starved man who has just seen food. Suddenly, a floodlight of understanding was all over me. I understood Jesus. A new lease of life was unleashed upon my soul. I realised something, the day I stopped trying so hard, the day I let go, was the day He started working mightily in me.

I started questioning almost everything I had known, and that was the beginning of losing friends and colleagues I had. I lost a church, friends and had relatives walk away. Though I also lost income, all that could not be compared to the treasure of God's love that constantly floods my soul. For the first time, miracles occur naturally without my effort. I'm now peaceful, happier and better focussed. I discovered, of course, that I was not the only one who understood the scriptures this way. God had lots of people all over the world passionately teaching these liberating truths in churches that meet in classrooms, underground, halls and rented premises while there were some other popular ministers who God had given a world impact on this message of grace.

My message is clear to you today. You could be in a situation like mine or even worse. Stop trying to please anyone. Jesus Christ is real. He is alive! Yes, He died, but He is risen. He has conquered the power of sin and the grave and death. He prevailed over Satan. He has established a New Covenant that ushers God's people into a life of overflowing grace and love. Sin can no longer have dominion over you because you are no longer under the old system but are under the New Covenant of God's grace. You don't need to be part of a big church nor a small church to be acceptable, Jesus Christ is enough. You just need to be part of a body of believers that affirm this truth that constantly points you to Jesus Christ. Believers who will always be vulnerable to the word of God and are not moved by the abilities of human beings but whose hope is constantly on Jesus Christ. The company of believers is necessary, though your completeness is independent of them. Constantly gazing at the Word and growing in the knowledge of Jesus is all you need to live a victorious life. It is possible to forgive and live a life of constant rest.

This life is a gift of God. If you have not received Jesus Christ in your heart, I take this opportunity to invite you to receive Him. Remember, this is a special relationship between you and a loving Father. After welcoming Him in your heart, He is so interested in helping you in every way possible. He desires to be so much in love with you. He will take away all bad things about you and you will realise over time that many of those things are no longer there as you continue to grow fellowship with Him. Stop trying to stop doing bad things. Keep growing in love and fellowship with the Father and He will do the rest. Proverbs 28:31NIV says "The wicked flee though no one pursues, but the righteous are as bold as a lion". The beauty is you don't have to do anything to be bold as a lion. Your loving father gives you righteousness as a precious gift (Romans 5:17) when you accept Him in your heart as Lord and Saviour. Receiving Jesus is the starting point of living this life of victory, a life of grace, a life of rest. If you are ready to receive eternal life, who is Jesus Christ, say this short prayer and believe, then you will be saved.

Dear Heavenly Father. Thank you for your love and for sending Jesus Christ to die for my sins. I believe in my heart that He died and rose again, defeating Satan and the power of sin. I accept this new life of God's Grace today, by confessing Jesus Christ as my own Lord and personal Saviour. Thank you, Father, for your love, grace and mercy. Thank you for calling me your child, in Jesus' precious name, Amen.

Congratulations! This simple prayer, according to Romans 10:8-10, coupled with your belief in your heart guarantees you to be a child of God. From now on, you can live a life of rest that this book was describing. 2 Corinthians 5:17 calls you a new creation. Your journey begins now. Get in touch using contact details in this book and prayerfully look for a place of fellowship where the truths shared in this book are taught.

Finally, in case you are already a believer or even a pastor like I was. You truly had a genuine salvation experience and probably received the baptism of the Holy Spirit with evidence of speaking in tongues. Maybe you have done some exploits for Jesus yet deep in your heart you know something is missing. I want to help you. Nothing is embarrassing by restoring your fellowship with the Father. If you are a pastor, nothing is embarrassing with correcting your doctrine or belief system by aligning it with Jesus. It takes humility.

Saul of Tarsus was passionately advocating for the keeping of the law. Passion never equals the truth. I had passion too. You may be passionate too. In case you have believed what you believe, for a long time; guess what? An untruth was spoken for generations never becomes the truth. The earth was once believed to be flat and that you could tip over if you get to the end of it. Today we know what the truth is. Jesus purchased a life of rest for you at Calvary. If your Christian life seems so hard, there is something wrong. Persecutions are there, yes, but we are joyful in them (Matthew 5:11-12 and James 1:2) because of this wonderful gift of God's rest. This hardness of Christianity you may be facing has nothing to do with persecutions of a believer but has everything to do with what you have believed. Christianity is the best life ever; you can live it again. I invite you to make a recommitment to the Lord. Deep in your heart, say this prayer:

> *Dear Heavenly Father, thank you for your love and grace. Thank you for the rest you purchased for me at Calvary. I ask that you, my glorious Father of our Lord Jesus Christ, that you give me spiritual wisdom and insight so that I might grow in the knowledge of God. I desire that Christ be fully formed in me. That I may fully understand His love and grace and eventually appropriate your life of rest without self-effort. I thank you, Lord, in Jesus name Amen.*

Congratulations and praise God for you. I want to direct you straight to the scriptures. Pick up a bible, any translation whose language you understand and start reading from the book of Romans and Galatians. Don't rush it. Read it slowly and prayerfully. Ask the Holy Spirit to reveal His truths. These books will affirm what Jesus did for you, the power you now have over sin and the place of the law under this covenant of God's grace. Read it for yourself. Over and over again! Ask questions. Don't just believe my word for it or even the word of a loved minister for it. Pick up the scriptures, and let the scriptures do all the work of interpreting scripture. Before long you will realise how simple the gospel is and how much it has been complicated and made to bring bondage. Labour in the Word to enter that rest.

I pray that the life of Jesus may constantly blossom in you and usher you to that place of rest where Jesus' perfect peace, that surpasses all understanding will constantly guide your thoughts and life. Stop trying and start living. Let that effortless, unforced rhythm of grace flow peacefully in you and through you.

Thank you for reading this book

For more information and other free ministry resources from Pastor Sbanga, connect with us on:

Web: https://PastorSbanga.Com

Facebook: https://fb.me/PastorSbanga

www.ingramcontent.com/pod-product-compliance
Lightning Source LLC
Chambersburg PA
CBHW071400290426
44108CB00014B/1633